# Rugby Disunion

## A Two-Part History
## of the formation of the
## Northern Union

## Trevor R. Delaney

First published in Great Britain in 1993 by Trevor R. Delaney, 6 Elmwood Terrace, Ingrow, Keighley, West Yorkshire BD22 7DP.

British Library Cataloguing-in-Publication Data.

A catalogue record of this book is available from the British Library.

ISBN 0-9509982-3-0

Printed by Thornton & Pearson (Printers) Ltd., Bradford.

# Contents

# Acknowledgements

I am particularly indebted to Robert Gate, the Rugby League's Archivist, who has kindly corrected the manuscript and has helped me with many other aspects of this publication.  For making available written material and photographs, I should also like to place on record my appreciation to the following: Timothy Auty, Paul Blackledge, Brian Cartwright, Tony Collins, John Jenkins, Rex King (Rugby Football Union Archivist), Michael Latham, Gladys Macek (The Wimbledon Lawn Tennis Museum), Dave Makin, Piers Morgan, Graham Morris, Dr Mark Nicholls (Cambridge University Library), Trevor Smith, Margaret Swarbrick (City of Westminster Archivist), David M. Watson (The Thoresby Society), Graham Williams, Cyril Willetts (Wednesbury Football Charity Association), and Peter Wynne-Thomas.  I also wish to thank Malcolm Heywood, Brian Walsh and all other staff of Thornton & Pearson (Printers) Ltd. involved in the production of this book, for their assistance, as well as numerous staff at the following reference libraries: Blackburn, Bradford, Castleford, Dewsbury, Durham, Halifax, Huddersfield, Keighley, Leeds, Oldham, and Wednesbury.

Trevor Delaney, Keighley, September, 1993.

*Back cover illustrations: the George Hotel, Huddersfield; Reverend Frank Marshall and James Miller; John Gallagher (London) tackles Martin Wood (Keighley) – (photograph Trevor Smith).*

# Introduction

There are many milestones in the history of rugby during the 19th century but, in relation to the present-day, none are more important than the rejection of broken-time at the Westminster Palace Hotel, Victoria Street, London, on 20 September, 1893, and the formation of the Northern Union at the George Hotel, Huddersfield, on 29 August, 1895.

Both events are so closely identified with each other that most rugby union historians have tended to look on them as being one and the same, appearing to believe that immediately following the first meeting the north's leading clubs broke away on the principle of broken-time. However, the defeat of Yorkshire's proposal, to compensate players for the wages lost whilst playing rugby, had no direct connection with the *"Great Schism"* two years later. It is in order to help destroy this myth, and to do justice to both subjects, that *Rugby Disunion* is in two parts, with this first volume ending immediately after the 1893 meeting.

Nevertheless, both crises clearly had their roots in the English class system and, to a great extent, in the different perceptions of life between the north and the south of England. Rugby's troubles erupted at a time of grave industrial strife, the early 1890s being marked by economic depression with disputes and strikes over wage rates and pay cuts. The mining areas of the north, and the worsted trade, centred in the West Riding of Yorkshire, were particularly badly hit. For example, in September, 1891, the Pilkington Brothers glass factory in St. Helens (the company also owned three pits) was set alight by striking miners; whilst the Manningham Mills (Bradford) strike from December, 1890 until April, 1891, ultimately led, in 1893, to the formation, in that same city, of the Independent Labour Party.

The Durham Light Infantry were the main force used to disperse the crowds on 14 April, 1891 in Bradford's Town Hall Square; and the deployment of the South Staffordshire Regiment at Lord Masham's Ackton Colliery at Featherstone on 11 September, 1893 resulted in eight miners being shot and two being killed. If proof were needed that it is impossible to detach sport from the overall fabric of society, perhaps one only need mention that three Bradford internationals - Fred Bonsor, Laurie Hickson, and Joe Hawkridge - were among the fifty special constables who were drafted in to assist the troops in the Bradford rioting, and consequently they found themselves baton charging the workers, many of whom, of course, were their own supporters.

But then, for most leading players, there was no shortage of work. Many local industrialists were also patrons of their town or city's rugby club, and even during recession there appears to have been little difficulty in finding employment for migrant Welshmen or players from the rural parts of the north. Westmoreland club, Kendal Hornets, quickly lost seven of its champion 9-a-side team to senior clubs in Lancashire and Yorkshire, and such *"importation"* or *"kidnapping"* was considered to be the cause of what was termed *"veiled professionalism"*. But, it was argued, was there anything wrong with a player utilising his rugby talents to improve his employment prospects in this way?

In so doing, however, he not only risked being suspended or banned for life, under the Rugby Union's professional regulations which were first introduced in 1886, but he also left himself open to coercion by club managers. It was not unknown, for example, for a player to be threatened with the sack for merely wishing to move club. Despite such *"tyranny"*, and the fact that the issue of broken-time was a major grievance with players, the working-class militancy in the workplace was not easily translated into organised player power, and certainly there was no organised players' union.

It seems that the personal ambition of most players was not to combine with others to demand improved match payments but to be installed as a publican and live off his reputation as a local sporting hero. This was one area which the Rugby Union's professional rules could not touch whilst, for the exceptionally-talented athlete, such as J. W. Sutcliffe (Heckmondwike to Bolton Wanderers), there was always the safe haven of professional soccer. Mere mortals, however, were less fortunate, with, in one case, the prize of a trouser length, in lieu of training expenses, being enough to lead to his suspension! It was not the fear of a players' revolt, therefore, which compelled the majority of clubs in Lancashire and Yorkshire to support the legalization of broken-time but the greater threat of full-time professionalism and the likelihood of extinction.

Although southerners generally were accused of not understanding these circumstances in the north, the greatest opposition to broken-time came from within Yorkshire itself. This was in the form of the Reverend Frank Marshall, who is the principal character in this first volume. He, and other amateur zealots like him, may well have believed that their victory in 1893 was cause for prolonged rejoicing, but, even today, rugby union has still not solved the problem of *"veiled professionalism"* or *"shamateurism"*, which first manifested itself over 100 years ago.

# Chapter One
# Reverend Frank Marshall, B.A.

Smoking a large Havana cigar, a stocky, bearded Muscular Christian stepped from the train at Huddersfield station. From a list of thirty candidates, the Reverend Francis Marshall had been appointed head of Almondbury Grammar School (founded by Charter of King James in 1609) and was arriving from the Black Country in time for the new term which was to start on 10 April, 1878. It is said that, *"He came with a reputation as an efficient organiser, a firm disciplinarian, a successful teacher, especially of mathematics, and a rugby fanatic".*[1] He would soon be joined from their home in Wednesbury by his widowed mother who was anticipating a peaceful retirement in the rolling Yorkshire hills.[2]

There would be little chance of this, however, as her son's distinctive appearance, and his rise to prominence - Yorkshire Rugby Union Treasurer in 1888/9 and 1889/90, Yorkshire President in 1890/1, and, from 1889/90 until September, 1892, a Yorkshire representative on the English Rugby Union committee - would make him one of the country's most easily identifiable sporting figures, who would court controversy both on and off the field.

As the north's leading referee, his eccentricity, of sometimes officiating whilst smoking a cigar, was occasionally frowned upon. But, it was as the leading opponent of broken-time, and chief prosecutor against *"professionalism"* that he proved to be most irksome. He later admitted that during the 1888/9 season he was under pressure from within the Huddersfield club committee to desist from pursuing such cases, although this did not stop him from bringing about the Fartowners' suspension (including, eventually, his own!) in 1893.[3]

Shortly after his unsuccessful attempt to prosecute neighbouring club Elland, the local youths of that town stoned the carriage carrying Marshall and his boys to an away game against Rishworth; and as Yorkshire President in 1891 he received many threatening letters from Oldham supporters after delving into their club's affairs. At the Roses match which followed, his presence in the stand at Fallowfield was seized upon by the rowdier spectators, one of whom was apparently overheard to shout, *"If Reverend Marshall sets foot in Oldham, he'll be shot!"* Marshall remained unruffled, however, and was said to have, *"smilingly observed them through his opera glasses".*[4] At the height of his rugby career, therefore, Frank Marshall would appear to have relished the limelight and the challenge. His strong convictions were supported by what he perceived as a clear mandate, which - shortly after Leeds St. John's, in 1889, became the first club nationally to be suspended for *"professionalism"* - he described as follows:

*The Yorkshire committee were called upon by the Yorkshire clubs, the public and by the press to put down professionalism...Those who accuse the committee or any member of it of partiality talk sheer and utter nonsense. Unfortunately I have myself come in for a good deal of "polite language"...but I do not care twopence what my assailants say of me. I do not feel offended or hurt. The offence is rather to those persons who have the imbecility and lowness to utter such remarks.*[5]

Although, during one of Marshall's long-winded after-dinner speeches, one player did overstep the mark by calling, *"Time, please!"*, and on another occasion he was howled down after making a speech in which he alluded to the infallibility of referees, the above abuse does not appear to have come from the players, with whom Marshall generally appears to have had a close affinity. At the end of the Scotland-England match in 1892, for example, he handed out cigars to the players as they left the field; and in many of the, admittedly nostalgic, player profiles he is spoken of with a certain amount of affection and respect, despite his reputation as a martinet.

As he became increasingly at odds with his Yorkshire colleagues, however - particularly from about 1892, when he upset the gate-taking clubs by his proposal that the proposed league should be sanctioned by the county - he began to rely heavily on the support of his southern allies, with whom he shared a similar educational and social background, as George F. Berney explained.

Note the language used by Berney - a former member of the Rugby Union Committee and past President of Surrey R.F.U. - to describe the broken-time proposal, whose advocates argued that it would actually delay the greater danger of full professionalism, against which they were also vehemently opposed:

*The earlier phases of the professional movement had disclosed Marshall as the living embodiment in Yorkshire of the Rugby Union spirit. He had set out to checkmate* (an apt metaphor in that Marshall was a member of the Huddersfield Chess Club) *the forces of evil, a task the fulfilment of which was grievously hampered by the hostility aroused by his unbending adherence to first principles and by difficulties now being experienced with those of his colleagues who had already become definitely converted to the broken-time theory. To a small*

*and intimate circle of friends in London on the occasions of his frequent visits to*
*the Metropolis, he used to reveal and explain the various moves that were being*
*engineered by the leaders of the professional cult for "capturing the machine".*[6]

Such clandestine work would achieve the success which Marshall and
the southern establishment desired; but it was not without considerable
personal sacrifice for himself and his wife, the daughter of an
Almondbury woollen manufacturer.[7]

Born at Hill Top, West Bromwich on  22 September, 1845, Francis
Marshall was educated at Brewood Grammar School, Staffordshire. He
was an undergraduate at St. John's, Cambridge from May, 1864, taking
First Class Honours in the Mathematical Tripos of 1868 and being
placed 38th in the class list.  That same year he was not only appointed
Vice-Principal of Carmarthen Training College but was ordained as
deacon of St. David's.  It says much for the old boy network that his
predecessor at Almondbury had also been Vice-Principal at Carmarthen,
where, incidentally, Marshall immediately set about forming the
college's first ever cricket club.[8]  It was in 1869 that he entered the
priesthood and from 1870 until 1878 was head of Wednesbury Collegiate
School, which may well have been his own private establishment.  He
proceeded to the MA degree in 1880 (although this involved no further
study at Cambridge); and his other academic work centred on a series of
educational text books on the Bible and mathematics which he
produced during his retirement.[9]

Marshall's most famous written work, however - in which,
incidentally, neither himself nor his fellow contributors make any
mention of William Webb Ellis - is undoubtedly that published in
1892.[10]  In it he meticulously recorded the transition of football from
the 13th century folk games - several of which, such as *"Uppies and*
*Downies"* at Workington, still survive today - laying great emphasis on the
contribution made by the public schools in codifying their various
games.

A history spanning 450 years, yet it was only weeks after Marshall's
18th birthday, in 1863, that the football world would fragment following
the formation of the Football Association, and during the next 15 years,
up to his arrival in Huddersfield, that other unprecedented
developments would occur.  Writing from the angle of Association
football, Percy Young has concluded that, *"Between 1863-1878 greater*
*changes took place in respect of the game than at any comparable period of time,*
*either before or since".*[11]

It would be impossible, of course, to apply this statement equally to
rugby.  Nonetheless, by 1878 - with common social improvements, such
as the Saturday half-holiday, increased spending power among the

9

working-class, and the spread of the railways; and with the establishment of a national governing body in 1871; the abolition of hacking and the reduction of teams from 20 to 15-a-side by 1875/6; the introduction of the Yorkshire Cup in 1877; and the formation of most of the north's senior clubs, including the future founder members of the Northern Union - most, if not all, of the groundwork had been laid, both for rugby's mass popularity in Lancashire and Yorkshire and its future conflicts.

Because of the small number of clubs in any one district, from the mid-1860s to the late 1870s, there was a need for players (and officials) to show a willingness to play (and help organise) under various rules, depending on the opposition. Some clubs, therefore, were formed with the original aim of promoting more than one code. The situation around Wednesbury, described by Frederick W. Hackwood on his return from college in 1872, was typical of this period, and helps explain why, as a young man, Reverend Marshall had to compromise in his choice of football. Hackwood stated:

*Football was practically unknown in the Wednesbury district, and nearly two years elapsed before a start of any kind could be made. At an early stage it had been recognised that the intricate Rugby code, to which I had been accustomed, would be quite impracticable for scratch teams....Turning my attention to the Association game I found that it was scarcely known outside the metropolis;....In this immediate locality there were too few in number to yield, by the arrangement of home and away matches, enough fixtures to fill up the whole season of Saturdays....*[12]

Hackwood therefore sent out a circular during August, 1873 inviting *"young gentlemen"* to help form a soccer club. Among the first to respond were Frank Marshall and Charles Henry Marshall, the latter, a solicitor and future Registrar at Holmfirth, near Huddersfield, who was to help his brother with his future rugby prosecutions, the sons of a tube manufacturer, a future Borough Surveyor, and the owner of a timber works. Therefore, with the help also of a number of headmasters in the district, on 6 September the Wednesbury Town F. C. was formed.

The following season they had local opposition from the Wednesbury Old Athletic, a club with its roots in the St. John's Night School. The wits in the town dubbed the Athletic *"The Hond Leathers"*, an allusion to the work gloves worn by these ironworkers, and Marshall's *"gentry"* side, *"The Kid Gloves"*.

For the opening of the 1876/7 season Town helped inaugurate Aston Villa's new ground at Perry Barr. Formed by cricket members of the Villa Cross Wesleyan Chapel, Villa's only game of the 1874/5 season had been against local Aston Brook St. Mary's rugby team - the first half under rugby rules and the second half under Sheffield Rules - and their rise to prominence can be directly attributed to the arrival in 1876 of two Scotsmen - George Ramsey, the club's first captain and secretary from 1884-1926, and William McGregor.[13]

The latter, an established draper who became the spokesman for the newly-formed Birmingham F.A., would not only lend his weight to the proposal in 1885 to legalise professionalism in soccer, but also would provoke the formation of the fully-professional Football League in 1888 when Aston Villa were one of the twelve founders. The other clubs, incidentally, were Accrington, Blackburn Rovers, Bolton Wanderers, Burnley, Everton, Preston North End - all from Lancashire - together with Stoke City, West Bromwich Albion, Wolverhampton Wanderers, Derby County and Notts County.

We have no record as to whether McGregor and Marshall actually met on that afternoon of 30 September, 1876, but with gate receipts a mere 5 shillings and three pence (26p) it is highly unlikely that any discussion would have focused on the need, or otherwise, for broken-time payments or full-time professionalism.

Almost certainly they would not have met on the field of play. At Cambridge Frank Marshall doubtless would have been influenced both by the kicking game under Cambridge Rules and rugby, which had been played there since 1861 - but there is no evidence to suggest that, other than as a student, he ever played either rugby or soccer. He was certainly an above average cricketer, however, having played for Wednesbury Cricket Club from 1873-75 but ill-health could well have been a cause of his non-participation in winter sport, for, despite his small stature, as a referee and umpire, he certainly could not have lacked courage.[14]

His brother, Charles, played against Wednesbury Literary and Athletic Institute on 16 January, 1875 when Frank was one of the umpires and on 6 February, 1875 a *"Marshall"* was in the side which played Moseley (formed by Havelock Cricket Club members in 1873) at rugby, soccer being played in the return fixture. We may safely assume that this was also Charles, as the club treasurer, Frank Marshall, was not included in the list of players in the 1877/8 annual report, which stated that he would be *"much missed as a most conscientious referee and umpire."*

At this time Wednesbury Old Athletic were the leading club in the Midlands and in deference to them Town had dropped the affix and became The Strollers. The *"Kid Gloves"*, however, upheld their past reputation by appearing in the final of the Birmingham Cup, only to lose to Shrewsbury F.C. at Aston Villa's Perry Barr on 6 April, 1878 - the game coinciding with Frank Marshall's departure to Yorkshire. Shortly before he left, he had umpired when his Wednesbury Collegiate School, who could muster only eight men, had beaten King Edward's Grammar School, Birmingham, in a game of soccer, which was reported in the *Midland Advertiser*. In response to an advertisement which Marshall placed in the same newspaper on 18 May, 1878 many of his former Wednesbury pupils, aged between 10 and 16 years, became boarders at Almondbury Grammar School, where his strict regime in winter included compulsory rugby every Thursday afternoon.

Almondbury Grammar Schools' ability at rugby would not greatly concern us were it not for the need to place it in context with the might of Yorkshire rugby. Because of bad weather only three games were played in 1888, including a defeat by Batley Grammar School by the mammoth score of 10 goals and 9 tries to nil. During 1889 the school won 6 of their 9 games, playing other Yorkshire grammar schools and Huddersfield College and in 1891, following "*continual practice under the supervision of Mr Lemm*", they won 9 of their 13 games against a similar level of opposition, including The Orphanage (Halifax) and Halifax Junior Clerks.[15]

Despite their low junior status, however, Almondbury Grammar School F. C. was a member of the Yorkshire and English Rugby Unions, and consequently had equal voting rights with the more prestigious gate-taking senior clubs.

The fixture against Huddersfield College had been discontinued as it had abandoned rugby in favour of lacrosse. Marshall was adamant, however, that, although lacrosse had taken root in parts of south-east Lancashire and had found favour with other rugby players in Yorkshire (including his future adversary and proposer of broken-time, James Miller) it would never cross the portal of Almondbury Grammar School whilst he was head. "*We do not think*", he rightly predicted, "*that lacrosse will take on long with Yorkshire lads as a substitute for the more robust and vigorous game of Yorkshire Rugby Football.*"

That he now saw rugby as the sole vehicle for the expression of his Muscular Christian views on rational recreation can be judged by the following brief extract, taken from the article which he wrote whilst addressing the question of broken-time:

*Why do I take the interest I do in this game? For the simple reason that I believe in the value of such a game in developing the physique, in influencing the character, and in improving the moral as well as the physical well-being of the working man player. It is emphatically a Saturday afternoon game; it is a game of little expense to the player, and therefore within the means of the working man both as to time and money, consequently no absolute necessity for the sacrifice of either work or money. And so I look upon football for the working man much as I regard the same game for my boys at school...(who)...whilst advancing in knowledge are at the same time developing their bodily frame and carrying out the wise maxim of "mens sana in corpore sano". They play for exercise and not for exhibition; and the same principle governs the main body of our gentleman players.*[16]

Most of the above assertions will come up for discussion later. For the moment, however, it is perhaps more appropriate to consider just how far Marshall had ostracised himself from the majority of Yorkshire opinion, and most of his former colleagues, judging from the following Yorkshire press comments, which appeared shortly after the broken-time meeting in 1893:

*One regrettable feature of the discussion was the personal feeling which one or two persons, who should have known better, went out of their way to introduce. The Reverend Frank Marshall, since his retirement from the Board of which he was formerly President, has so often been in opposition to his old colleagues that an exception on this occasion would have come as somewhat in the nature of a surprise. Some of his remarks, however, had neither the justification of relevancy, nor the merit of good taste. When, too, he charged the Yorkshire Rugby Union with introducing a "Relief Bill" by means of which they could evade the penalties of professionalism, he made a statement we rather fancy he would have as much difficulty in substantiating as he has in the past had in proving that his suspicions against certain clubs and players were well grounded. It is one thing to repeat the idle and irresponsible gossip of the dressing-room; it is quite another to make a serious charge against honesty and good sportsmanship and prove it. So far the representative of the Almondbury Grammar School F.C. has not been quite successful in discriminating between the two.*[17]

And a contemporary was equally as scathing, both of Marshall, and the system of voting which gave him his influence:

*But what are we to think of the Reverend F. Marshall? I yield to no one in my admiration of the past work of this gentleman in Yorkshire....His own remarks....demonstrate clearly enough that he is only too well aware of the danger of us drifting into absolute professionalism. Why then should he adopt such an antagonistic attitude?....Is the essence of all that is purely amateur in Yorkshire football incarnated in the Reverend F. and his boys at Almondbury? He might recently have convinced himself on that point, but the majority of those interested in the game in this county beg to differ....Is it not somewhat ridiculous that the master of the Almondbury Grammar School Club should have as much power in a division....as say, the representatives of Bradford, Leeds, Halifax or other large clubs whose followers are numbered in thousands?....Here is the Reverend F. Marshall taking a prominent part in opposition to the vast majority of football patrons in the county, and on what ground? As the representative of himself and a school which if it ceased to exist today would cause no anxiety or inconvenience, would scarce ever be missed. The question of representation needs serious consideration, and had the voting on payment for broken-time been calculated on the basis of club membership or gate money the result of the voting would have been vastly different.*[18]

In 1878, such matters were blissfully absent from rugby discussions. Equally, the arrival in Huddersfield of a squat cleric from the Midlands was the cause of no public curiosity. As he climbed aboard a handsome cab in the station forecourt for the next stage of his journey to the heights of Almondbury, Reverend Marshall caught his first sight of the impressive St. George's Square, including The George Hotel, the latter being the Huddersfield club's headquarters and the future birthplace of the Northern Union.

He could hardly have envisaged that some 15 years hence - only weeks after the rejection of broken-time - this same cobbled expanse would be filled by crowds awaiting the announcement of Huddersfield's suspension, in consequence of which - with his power in Yorkshire rugby effectively over - he would qualify as the most unpopular person in town. Nor could he have foreseen that, shortly after the split in rugby, he would have to leave Aldmondbury, and his career in teaching, under something of a cloud.

# Chapter Two
# The North-South Divide?

Shortly after Frank Marshall arrived in Huddersfield sporting values in Lancashire and Yorkshire began to mirror the harsh competitiveness of that area's industrial life. Many industrialists had either helped form, or were patrons of, the local rugby club, and, although they certainly did not seek to directly benefit financially from their club interests, nonetheless they brought their entrepreneurial skills to the rugby market place.

The huge levels of public support in these two counties - attendances at many *"ordinary"* matches exceeded those at internationals in London - fuelled what was termed *"veiled professionalism"*, with employment (the public house was favourite) and other material inducements being offered to players to transfer their services, both from local clubs and those in other parts of the British Isles.

Leading up to the crucial meeting in the 1893 it therefore appears to be a relatively simple exercise to compare the nature of rugby north and south of the River Trent - a dividing line which the Northern Union would use to mark out its initial territory. Yorkshire and Lancashire dominated the national rugby scene from the commencement of the official county championship in 1888/9. There were significant differences in attitude between the north and the south towards this Championship, as well as towards the importance of league and cup competitions, success in the latter being the catalyst for a wave of community and civic rejoicing. The formation of leagues by the north's leading gate-taking clubs in 1892/3 was, in fact, anathema to the southern establishment, as this development was not only seen as a potential means of side-stepping the authority of the county unions, but was considered to be the precursor of full-time professionalism. The seriousness with which the game was pursued in the north is also indicated by the earlier start to the season; the greater number of fixtures; and the introduction of special diets for players and the appointment of professional trainers before major matches.

Many of the incidents of crowd violence and referee baiting were attributable to the high level of public betting, associated with which were a number of (unsubstantiated) allegations that players were actually *"throwing"* games. Though relatively minor and isolated at this stage, there were also some indications of players being in dispute with club managements, over what might be termed conditions of service.

Such was the sharply contrasting nature of the game in these two areas of the country that gentleman rugby tourists from the deep south could perhaps have been excused for thinking that they had entered a different land.

The broken-time issue appears to epitomise the feeling of northern alienation from the Rugby Union's southern-based decision makers. Other grievances included Yorkshire's under-representation on the national committee; the failure to hold meetings in the north or at times that were convenient for northern delegates to attend meetings in London; the perceived bias towards the selection of southern players for internationals and the failure to keep pace with the demands of the game in the north by a reluctance to introduce such improvements as penalty laws for off-side and a simplified and equitable scoring system by points. The Rugby Union's failure to bring the international dispute to a speedy conclusion also raised the hackles of many northerners.

Regardless of the above, however, in terms of sheer numbers, the northern clubs were in a very powerful position in September, 1893, when the Yorkshire proposal for broken-time was considered at the general meeting of the Rugby Union. At that time, well over half of all the clubs in membership of the Rugby Union came from the north of England.

The above *prima facie* evidence would therefore seem to support the view that a north-south divide existed in rugby long before the broken-time meeting in 1893, and that, because of the greater voting strength in the north at that time, and the general apathy of the southerners, there was every possibility that broken-time payments would be legalised. But, as we shall endeavour to prove in this and other chapters, such a simple assessment is fraught with problems.


If Frank Marshall had peered to his right on approaching Huddersfield he would have noticed a symbolic development. For there on the hillside work had started on enlarging the Fartown (St. John's) cricket enclosure and laying-out a rugby pitch. Other than the pavilion, the facilities were still very basic but these changes signified, not only the game's strong ties with cricket, but the fact that, in this part of the world, rugby was about to become a major spectator sport.

Rugby's first appearance in the town was in 1865 when Leeds Athletic and Manchester helped propagate the game to, among others, the Huddersfield Athletic Club, one of whose founder members was the father of Huddersfield's first international, Harry Huth. Although it amalgamated with St. John's Cricket Club in 1875, the rugby section continued to play at the Rifle Field (now Greenhead Park) whilst the above-mentioned alterations were made in time for the game against Manchester Rangers on 2 November, 1878, which Reverend Marshall most likely attended as a fully paid up member.

At that time the cricket and rugby fields had a common boundary and there were tennis courts behind an *"unsightly wooden structure"* which masqueraded as a grandstand. Fartown, however, was considered to be a suitable venue for the Blackburn Rovers - Sheffield Wednesday F.A. Cup semi-final on 6 March, 1882. The attendance of 10,000 pleased the soccer authorities, who were then attempting to gain a foothold in what remained (outside the Sheffield and Barnsley area) a rugby-orientated West Riding until 1903.[1]

The reason for rugby's dominance was due, almost entirely, to the success of the Yorkshire Cup, the first final of which, in December, 1877, had been scheduled for the Rifle Field. It was the nearest that rugby came to equalling the F. A.'s nationwide contest and it was to play a crucial role in the commercialisation of the game in Yorkshire and in exposing the nature and issue of *"veiled professionalism"*. Before examining this upsurge in rugby's popularity, however, we need to briefly consider how there came to be two rival codes of football, and how rugby was established in the north, with particular emphasis on Lancashire and Yorkshire.

Reverend Marshall reminded his readers in 1892 that the game had evolved from those played at the great English public schools, *"It is well to emphasise this fact in these days when the enthusiastic supporters of the game in the North are apt to forget the source from which the game has sprung and are ready to imagine that all interest in the game and (its) development are the peculiar prerogatives of the sport-loving public of Yorkshire and Lancashire. It should never be forgotten"*, he lectured, *"that the schools taught the game and that the old school boys created football clubs."* [2] That was certainly true in many cases, but, unfortunately, when discussions opened on the prospect of having one universal game, ex-public schoolboys had naturally tended to remain loyal to their particular school rules.

It was in response to this need for a unified code of football that six meetings were held at the Freemason's Tavern, Lincoln's Inn Fields, London, during 1863. At the first meeting of the Football Association (F.A.) in October eleven clubs from the capital were represented. The new *"Cambridge Rules"*, which had been drawn up earlier that month, prohibited *"running in"* and *"hacking"* - the latter being the practice of kicking an opponent's shins if they got in the way of the ball - and, although the early meetings had favoured these characteristics of the game played at Rugby School, by the fifth meeting there was an open disagreement between the two sides. F. W. Campbell of Blackheath, which was founded in 1858 by old boys of Blackheath Proprietary School, and referred to with an air of superiority as *"The Club"* - had argued that the proposed rules would *"emasculate"* football and this led to their withdrawal from the F. A. Campbell, however, continued as treasurer of the F. A. for some time after.[3]

The north had been omitted from these crucial discussions in 1863 although there were certainly a few clubs in Lancashire and Yorkshire, apart from those at educational establishments, which could have been invited. A rugby club, composed initially of Old Rugbeians, was established in Liverpool in 1857 following an exhibition game; and, likewise, a game in 1860 between Old Rugbeians and ex-Cheltenham College pupils was responsible for the formation of the exclusive Manchester club

Manchester controlled Lancashire's county's affairs - with the help of Liverpool - until agitation by Broughton, Manchester Rangers, Free Wanderers, Swinton, and Birch led to the formation of the Lancashire County Football Club on 22 December, 1881, at which Walton, Rossendale, Oldham, Manchester Athletic, Rochdale Hornets, Chorley, and Cheetham were also represented.

The South East Lancashire Union (formed 1877) and West Lancashire Union (formed 1884), with 41 and 23 clubs respectively by 1892, were both affiliated to this county authority. The West Lancashire Union was made up of the senior clubs, which would give almost one hundred percent support to Yorkshire's proposal for broken-time. The one exception was Broughton, one of whose founder members was John Henry Payne, the Lancashire cricketer and the former international half-back, who was the county's secretary and treasurer in 1893.

The mutual arrangement of fixtures allowed the socially exclusive clubs to avoid contact with their social inferiors. By 1890, however, this policy was beginning to have an adverse effect on the Mancunians, and after a heavy defeat by Bradford it was reported:

*Poor Manchester!...Slowly but surely (it is) going down the hill to extinction and unless there is more popularisation in its management it will soon become a fitting opponent for a Yorkshire back-yard fifteen.*

When leagues were introduced in 1892/3, however, Manchester, together with every club in Liverpool, remained aloof and, along with

18

Broughton, who later dropped out of league competitions and were defunct by 1894/5, were at the forefront of opposition to broken-time.

Across the Pennines, the only known football club before the 1860s was Sheffield F.C., which is considered to be the world's oldest, having issued its constitution and own set of eleven playing rules on 24 October, 1857. Most members were ex-pupils of Sheffield Collegiate School and members of Sheffield Cricket Club at Bramall Lane, which had been opened in April, 1855. By 1862 there were 15 clubs playing in the district under the Sheffield Rules.[4]

Considering that there was no rugby club in the city at that time, it is surprising to find that Sheffield supplied no fewer than five players for the first, 20-a-side, Roses rugby match on 28 March, 1870 - especially when one considers that W. H. H. Hutchinson, an Old Rugbeian and Hull and Yorkshire's first rugby international, had to tell one of these Sheffield men that hitting an opponent on the head with the ball was not allowed![5]

Liverpool and Manchester players made up the Lancashire team that day whilst Yorkshire were also represented by Bradford, Leeds Athletic (formed in 1864), Hull, York, and Huddersfield, who formed *"The Yorkshire County Football Club"* in 1874. In 1884 they allowed Halifax, Dewsbury, Leeds St. John's, Wakefield Trinity, and Thornes to join, and promised future winners of the Yorkshire Cup a seat but it was not until 1888 that the county body became fully democratic through representation by districts.

The first Bradford club, which then played a mixture of rugby and association with no handling allowed except for a fair catch, was launched in 1866, although the founding group of ex-Bramham College and Steeton College pupils under the leadership of Oates Ingham of the Lingfield Dyeworks, Thornton Road, had played their first informal games in 1863 on Horton cricket ground. They merged with Bradford Cricket Club (formed 1836) in time for the opening of Park Avenue in 1880 to become the richest and strongest club in the country.

A fixture against Bradford was much sought after as they could offer large match guarantees and lavish hospitality. In 1886 they became the first Yorkshire club to entertain Blackheath and their later rift with the *"Heathens"*, over the latter's match expenses, would not only epitomise the notion of a north-south divide but act as a portent of the pending split in the Union.

Hull had been formed in 1865 by a wine and spirit merchant, a local solicitor, and the above-mentioned W. H. H. Hutchinson, who was the head of a steamship company. Early members included a number of ex-public schoolboys from Marlborough, Cheltenham College and St.

Peters School, York; and Reverend John Scott, who also organised the Rifle Volunteer Force, and his five sons. Hull first played at the home of Gilbert Harrison, partner in Harrison Brothers, corn merchants.

They had great difficulties in arranging local rugby fixtures - having to compromise by also playing under association rules against such as Bramham College and Lincolnshire clubs - but they could always rely on games with St. Peter's, York, however, some of whose former pupils, including Robert H. Christison, formed the first club in the Minster City under their original title of York Amateurs. Whilst York hold the honour of contesting the first Yorkshire Cup final it is Hull F.C. who have the distinction of being the first Yorkshire club to join the Rugby Union - a governing body which was desperately needed by the end of the 1860s for a variety of reasons.

The fact that certain clubs in the capital were playing to their own amended rules made it imperative that a central controlling authority should be established. London clubs, for example, tended to throw in (as today) opposite to where the ball crossed the touchline, as distinct from the Rugby School rule of where the ball first hit the ground in touch; and in 1866 Richmond (a club originally formed under Harrow rules) prohibited hacking, and, ironically, together with Blackheath refused to play against clubs which still used what the latter now belatedly accepted as being a barbaric practice.

The public outcry against the dangers of hacking (there was the death of a Richmond player in a practice match), and the progress being made by the F.A. - who had the audacity to stage a Scotland versus England international at the Oval, although nearly all the Scottish clubs at that time played rugby - were given as the main reasons for the Rugby Union's formation in 1871. On 26 January, at the Pall Mall Restaurant, Regent Street, members of twenty London and surburban clubs (the Wasps representative, apparently, could not find the hotel) elected a committee, seven of whom were Old Rugbeians, under the Presidency of E.C. Holmes, the captain of Richmond. The original members (Blackheath, Harlequins, Richmond, Civil Service, Wellington College, Guy's Hospital, King's College, and St. Paul's School, which are still in existence, and Marlborough Nomads, West Kent, Wimbledon Hornets, Gypsies, Clapham Rovers, Law, Flamingoes, Queen's House (formed 1867 defunct by 1892), Lausanne, Addison, Mohicans, and Belsize Park, which are all now defunct) adopted the laws of Rugby School, but minus hacking and a few other minor amendments.

It was perhaps no coincidence that the rival F.A. should be prompted to introduce their national knock-out competition later that same year, when both Civil Service and Lausanne were among the clubs which voted for the proposal at the F.A. meeting on 16 October, 1871.

With four public schools represented, together with others from the professions, the Rugby Union's initial social make-up was therefore decidedly from the public school elite, if the England side which took part in the first international against Scotland on 27 March, 1871 is any guide.[6] Manchester and Liverpool supplied six members of this, although they did not join the Rugby Union until this body decided that only players from member clubs would be selected for internationals.

The lack of recognition of northern players outside of these exclusive Lancashire clubs was to be a major irritant to supporters, who once voiced their disapproval in a most novel way. At the first international to be played in Yorkshire - at Cardigan Fields, Leeds, in 1884 - the locals on the popular stand had the answer to this neglect by sarcastically encouraging and applauding the England players, not by their real names, but by substituting the names of their favourite Tykes!

Although it later became increasingly impossible for Yorkshire players to be overlooked for internationals (there were eight Yorkshiremen in the side which beat the Maoris in February, 1889 and a similar number against Scotland in 1892), notwithstanding the usual criticisms aimed at selectors, the feeling persisted that there was a social and geographical bias in many of the international selections. One example of this was when Huddersfield's Jack Dyson, *"a working man"*, was said to have been unfairly dropped in favour of Blackheath's Andrew Stoddart, *"a toff"*, against Ireland in 1890.

This acrimony would reach its peak in 1895 when, after the 36-0 defeat of the north by the south, Yorkshire was totally overlooked - except for the late inclusion of T. H. Dobson - for the deciding game of the international championship. Based on the above result, the southerners obviously expected England to win, but Scotland had other ideas, and following England's defeat one northern correspondent ventured the opinion:

*By this match the Rugby Union have had the oft taught lesson forced home to them, that in order to successfully resist the efforts of the brawny Scots the English scrimmage must have a sprinkling of Yorkshiremen. In 1890 and 1892 when England were successful Yorkshire supplied the backbone of the pack and to them alone was due whatever honour was attached to winning the game.*[7]

Though not responsible for this selection blunder in 1895, if one man could be said to have epitomised the southern-based Rugby Union, it was (Sir) George Rowland Hill. In 1867, his brother, Captain E. Cleary Hill, had formed Queens House, which was named after the family residence at Greenwich, and it was with this club that Rowland Hill played as half-back, and was first elected, in 1879, onto the Rugby Union committee. Two years later he became that body's honorary secretary, a post which he held until 1904.

He was born in the precincts of the Naval School at Greenwich, where his father, Reverend James Hill, the headmaster of the Royal Hospital Upper School, was chaplain. Educated at Christ's Hospital, as a 15-year old he was employed in laying telegraph cables in the Atlantic, a job he soon left due to his dislike of the sea. From there he was appointed to the Principal Probate Registry at Somerset House where he held the position of Record Keeper for many years until his retirement. Chairman of the Greenwich Conservative Party for 30 years - *"amateur of amateurs and Tory of Tories"* as *The Times* obituary described him - it was said, elsewhere, that he loved nothing better than *"to harangue the working-man on the leading topics,"* during his time on London County Council.

As Rugby Union secretary he was considered to be more of a *"Premier"* than a secretary, whose opinions were greatly respected. G. F. Berney described this influence and his oratorical powers thus:

*By nature he is a calm man but there is something more to tell....The power he wields at general meetings is evident the moment he rises. As he warms to his subject he electrifies his audience, and on occasions of great moment he has been known almost to drown friend and foe together in the rushing torrent of his peroration. But the man is unconscious of it all.*[8]

Needless to say, his opposition to broken-time carried substantial weight.

Rowland Hill was also the game's most proficient and widely-travelled referee. He was generally well respected, but, nonetheless, after refereeing the 1884 Yorkshire Cup final which went off with little trouble, at the Lancashire-Cumberland game at Whitehaven in 1891 a crowd disturbance against him resulted in Cumberland's county fixtures being moved away from the town. Some of his decisions also upset the Maoris in 1889, resulting in three of their side walking off the field against England. This impetuous behaviour was perhaps excusable, however, as the rules presented enormous problems to even the most experienced of players and officials.

The original (20-a-side) game drawn up by the Rugby Union - with its 59 Laws as opposed to the F.A.'s 14 in 1863 - was according to Reverend Marshall, *"....so delightfully vague as to be capable of interpretation only by those thoroughly imbued with the spirit thereof, and who had played from boyhood"*. So vague, in fact, that such an expert as the Scottish headmaster, H. H. Almond, had to confess that in the first England-Scotland international in 1871, although he was one of the umpires, he still could not say on what grounds England's appeal against the winning *"pushover"* try had been turned down! These were the days when - aided and abetted by umpires - much depended on the honourable conduct of the captains to decide on points of dispute.

The neutral referee, first employed in 1885, was not given sole control of the game in England until the broken-time meeting in 1893 - shortly after the Welsh had introduced the innovation. Because clubs were sometimes reluctant to appoint referees, particularly for second teams fixtures, it was not uncommon for disagreements to last as long as ten to fifteen minutes, which inevitably led to a number of unsavoury incidents with spectators. Problems for referees were apparently not unique to the north, as Rowland Hill, in his address to the 4th annual London Society of Referees in October, 1892, said that, *"Players' criticisms of referees' decisions was almost a disease. Clubs should bear the cost of the referee's expenses but they don't even get a thank you and clubs were simply not supplying men to help the society."*

As penalty kicks were considered to be undesirable among gentlemen, such practices as *"wing-forward"* and other off-side play went unpunished until 1882 when the 5-yard rule was introduced. Even so, when there was no referee the rule was impossible to implement - and, even when it was, a goal from such a penalty was not allowed until 1888/9. Ironically, one effect of the abolition of hacking had been to reduce the game to long *"shoving matches"* among the forwards, and any passing that did occur was confined to the half-backs and forwards, with half-back play consisting of drop-kicking to touch or at goal or individual sprints for the line.

At the meeting of the Yorkshire Rugby Union Referees' Society in December, 1892, at which the new laws were under discussion, the Yorkshire President, James A. Miller, stated that the reduction of teams to 15-a-side in 1875/6 greatly improved playing standards and the game as a spectacle. Having played as a 13-year old with Leeds Middle Class School, and having represented Yorkshire as a forward in 1879 and 1881 before taking up refereeing, Miller - who was also Yorkshire's secretary from 1884 - was well able to judge. However, the first pass by a half to a threequarter - J. H. Payne (Broughton) to C. E. Bartram (Wakefield Trinity) - was apparently not made until the North versus South match of 1881, and it was not until 1886 that Bradford's three-quarter Rawson Robertshaw was said to have introduced the innovation of a service to his winger. Furthermore, the Welsh four-threequarter system was not established in England until at least 1893/4. The laws of the game had been revised for the start of 1892/3 season to only 20 clauses, but they were still apparently *"....far from lucid, and certainly would be unintelligible to anyone but a player of some experience"*. It is therefore small wonder that at

23

the above meeting James Miller should advocate such a revolutionary step as reducing rugby union to 13-a-side. The future proposer of broken-time was perhaps the first person to favour this step - fourteen years before it was introduced into rugby league in 1906/7.

This slow evolution of the old schoolboy game was galling for northern officials who had to administer what was quickly becoming a mass spectator sport. Their frustration in those days, faced with crowd disturbances, and the threat posed by professional soccer, was perhaps summed up by the comments made by a Yorkshire editor some years later:

*As a matter of fact the Board has never shown a disposition to deal frankly and fully with any suggested reforms emanating from Yorkshire. Take the agitation of 1881 with the suggested penalties for off-side and the proposed system of scoring by points, and what do we find? Why, that although the action taken by Yorkshire was a measure distinctly forced upon them by the framers of the rules, yet the proposition was overwhelmingly defeated. Thus it was the infringement of the laws increased year by year, the public in the meantime enacting scenes which no one could regard but anything but sorrow. It was Yorkshire, however, which made herself heard in the long run and it was she and not the supine Rugby Union who brought the crusade to an end; and also with regard to the system of scoring by points. This question was also one of principle; but still it took several seasons to secure an alteration, both with respect to this and other matters relating to the better government of the game...*[9]

Prior to referees using a whistle and the umpires flags (which apparently was not until the North versus South game at Bradford in 1885/6) there were endless hold-ups because of the difficulty in letting players know that an appeal had been made, and *"fraudulent 16th man"* umpiring persisted until 1889 when they were assigned to touch-line duties. It was because of the problems with rule interpretations that the international dispute, which saw England ostracised by the other home countries, arose in the 1884; and Reverend Marshall himself had to acknowledge that he had overstepped his powers in ordering a touch-judge from the field of play during a local cup-tie in 1890.

It was little wonder, therefore, that around the time of the Rugby Union's formation, the number of clubs - not including the local grammar schools and public schools - was few in the North. A. M. Crook (Free Wanderers) said that:

*About the year 1870 properly constituted organisations in Lancashire could be counted on the fingers of one hand and in many instances, with a free and open gate, matches were played before handfuls of spectators, these being mostly friends of the combatants...Gate-money, the most demoralising factor of modern rugby...was almost unknown whilst the Press was not interested in this new branch of sport.*[10]

Although the first Roses match pre-dates the formation of the Rugby Union, the picture was much the same in Yorkshire, where it was said that, prior to the inauguration of the Yorkshire Cup, editors were unwilling to publish reports of club games, and there was no demand for other literature on the game. This is borne out by the *Yorkshire Post* claiming, rightly or wrongly, that they were the first national newspaper, in 1879, to report daily on the game. This apathy towards rugby in the early 1870s was not due entirely to the rules, but more to the fact that the working man had so far been denied access to it, both as a player and a spectator, due to the Saturday afternoon shift not finishing until at least 2 p.m.

It was the operatives centred in the cotton and woollen textile industries of Lancashire and the West Riding of Yorkshire - in the very areas where rugby was to achieve initial dominance - who were the first group of workers nationally to achieve the Saturday half-holiday, when in 1874 Parliament lowered the number of hours from 60 to 56 and a half. This meant ten hours work (excluding meal breaks) Monday to Friday and six and a half hours on Saturday, finishing at one o'clock.[11]

For the first time, therefore, the working man was freed from the drudgery and dangers of the workplace on Saturday afternoons, and thus able to take up sport. Although other groups of workers soon benefited from these shorter hours the legislation did not include such as clerks and shop assistants. It was not until Tuesday, 6 October, 1885, for instance, that the Drapers met the Grocers to celebrate the first day of half-day closing in Keighley, and during the same season there was a proliferation of teams associated with clerks and tradesmen - for example, Leeds Telegraph Clerks met their namesakes from York.

If such a dangerous game as rugby (deaths resulting from playing injuries were almost a weekly occurrence) could hold sway over soccer among such workers, it therefore had little difficulty in finding enthusiasts among the more macho occupations. During the 1870s and early 1880s farming produced its fair share of players, and there were clubs in Durham closely associated with steelworks and dock workers. Clubs also sprang up throughout the north-east, Lancashire and south Yorkshire coalfields. A club was formed in 1877 in Castleford, a town, which - like St. Helens - had glassmaking as its original core industry, but which later also became closely identified with mining. Of all the manual occupations, it was mining which became synonymous with the game in the north, to the extent that the association of mine shafts and rugby league was to become a well-worn cliché.

There are clear dangers in readily accepting such regional

stereotypes, nonetheless, we perhaps need to accept that, at the time of the broken-time meeting, the north owed its strength to the fact that players in working-class occupations had either formed their own clubs or had been readily accepted into existing club memberships. A study of clubs in Rochdale shows that the former was perhaps the rule rather the exception during the 1880s. Other research has revealed that clubs such as Rochdale Hornets and Hull - where the latter had allowed into its membership by 1871 a plumber, a glazier and a gas fitter - differed socially from most clubs in and around London.[12]

It was generally accepted that in those southern counties most players had learned the game whilst at school. Whatever advantages, physical or otherwise, that the working-class player might have possessed, Reverend Marshall had no doubts about the benefits of this early schooling in the game:

*Besides, in our manufacturing towns and villages in the north the class of player is very different from his compeer in the south. The southern players have for the most part graduated in the science of the game at school, and many of them afterwards at one or other of the Universities. Such a course of football education can have only one result, viz. that the player is impregnated with the spirit of the game....this will perhaps account for the finish and style of most southern teams.*

*But in the north the case is different. A few years ago in such clubs as Manchester and Huddersfield, both then powers in the land, the public school element was to the front and the introduction of the working class element not an accomplished fact, but first county contests, and then the Yorkshire Challenge Cup lent such a stimulus to the game that clubs came into existence on every side....*[13]

It was that public school "*style*", incidentally, which Blackheath would accuse Bradford of lacking at the time of the southerners' dispute over expenses.

The fact that the working man also had surplus spending power to add to his increased leisure time on Saturday afternoons provided the other important ingredient to this upsurge in popularity, namely, the birth of the partisan spectator. One hesitates to say "paying spectator" as most early grounds were on common land or unfenced publicans', farmers' or landowners' fields where whatever money was taken was by way of a voluntary collection. The first match at which Swinton made an admission charge, for example, was on 7 March, 1874 against Moss Side Grasshoppers; whilst Wigan's first secretary, in 1881, recalled making some collection boxes similar to the ones used in churches. His experience taught him that those spectators beyond the ropes did not bother to lean over and deposit a donation and he therefore decided to tack on a four foot handle in order to reach them! During this period, therefore, most clubs were not yet ready to take advantage of the game's commercial potential, but this would soon change with the pressure on the leading clubs to enclose their grounds and erect grandstands, coinciding with the increasing popularity of the various cup competitions. As with Fartown, many grounds in the north, particularly in Yorkshire, would be multi-purpose.[14]

As we have seen, some of the early rugby clubs in the north obviously owe their formation to the pioneering work of ex-public schoolboys. A large number, however, were dependent upon long-established local organisations, whose members, for a variety of motives, sought to add a winter game to their activities.

Barlow's study in Lancashire, and an analysis of clubs in the Yorkshire Rugby Union handbook for 1883/4, would indicate, however, that most could be identified by their district or street locality - Kildwick Parish, and Heckmondwike Church Street Roughs, for example. More exclusively, a club at Badsworth (population 742 in 1881), which took part in the second Yorkshire Cup in 1879, was formed by members of the local hunt.

In the northern part of West Yorkshire - where soccer clubs struggled to gain anything like an organised presence until the formation of the West Yorkshire League in 1894 - evidence would cast doubt on the assumption that, because of the game's greater roughness, the church was less interested in promoting rugby as opposed to soccer in the 1870s and 1880s.[15] Although it is not yet known whether the initiatives came from the clergy or the church members, at least 15% of the sample survey of over 200 Yorkshire clubs, which appeared in the 1883/4 fixtures, were still identifiable with a church or chapel. This percentage, however, was almost certainly understated as such as Bradford junior club, Bowling (formerly Bowling St. John's), had by this time dropped their suffix. This perhaps coincided not only with their rejection of Muscular Christian values, but the need for the club to be widen their area of public appeal on moving their ground away from the vicinity of the church.

Many other senior clubs are also known to have been patronised by the local clergy. The forerunner of the present Leeds rugby league club, Leeds St. John's, was formed in 1870 by four members of the St. John the Evangelist Sunday school cricket team, which included their first captain and county player, Tom J. Ogden, M.A. The future head of Park Hurst Preparatory School, Buxton, Ogden played rugby in glasses and was often found searching for these on the pitch during a game!

St. John's first game was against the original Wakefield club on the cinders of the Militia Barracks at Carlton Hill, when they played one half under rugby and the other under association rules. The first balance sheet shows that Reverend C. Houlbrook made a half-crown donation in the total income of £1/9/6d but he apparently played no active part in the club's formation. The afore-mentioned James A. Miller joined the club shortly after leaving school, at which time Kirkstall St. Stephens was said to be one of the few other clubs in the city.

Other church connections with northern rugby clubs are to found in Wakefield Trinity (formed 1870), Salford (originally formed under the title of Cavendish F.C. in 1873, by members of Cavendish Street Chapel Sunday School, Hulme), Heckmondwike (formed in the early 1870s by Reverend W. T. Storrs and Reverend J. C. Blackburn), Radcliffe (formed in 1875 as the Radcliffe Close Wesleyan F. C., Runcorn (formed in 1876 as a section of the Runcorn Young Men's Christian F.A. Athletic Club), Keighley (formed in 1876 as a soccer and rugby club under the Presidency of Reverend F. Marriner, Bramley (formed in 1879 at a meeting presided over by the Parish vicar) and, around that same year, Leeds Parish Church recreation club added a rugby section, for which Reverend E. H. Dykes, Reverend Bierley, and Reverend H. T. Heygate all gave yeoman service.

Nationally, the Muscular Christians may well have been less interested in rugby because of its inane roughness, but in West Yorkshire they most certainly attempted to promote the game with which their working-class Parishioners most identified. What perhaps needs further research is the following assertion that the clergy and other professional classes were driven out of playing Yorkshire rugby by the rough play and unruly crowd behaviour of their social inferiors:

*Who with any experience of the pleasant and enjoyable time does not look back with regret to the period when a football match was a healthy sport and amusement, and not a serious business and occupation? Why are so few public schoolmen and clergymen found in our leading fifteens? It is because the associations of the game are becoming thoroughly distasteful to any gentlemen of sportsmanlike feelings. They do not care to be hooted, and yelled at as part and parcel of a sixpenny show or to meet and associate with men who care nothing for the game except as a means to an end.*[16][27]

Was this really a true reflection of the situation, however, or did it merely prove the point, made by a contemporary, that, *"The latter-day cant on the subject of old-time football is founded largely on sentiment."* Were not the clergy and ex-public school players simply being replaced by working-class players, who soon became more proficient at the game?

Apart from the church, rugby's development in the north owed a great deal to such as the volunteer regiments, and athletic and cricket club members. As we shall see in future chapters, cricket was not without influence as regards introducing many rugby players to the

28

culture of financial and material rewards from sport and neither was the power which was wielded by the north's leading local industrialists.

Not only did the *"Great and the Good"* help form several clubs, but, as local employers, and, in some cases, civic leaders, and Freemasons, their patronage paved the way for the importation of players from neighbouring clubs and other parts of the British Isles. This process will be revealed in the inquiries into alleged cases of professionalism, when it should soon become apparent that, of all the northern sporting families, the Newsome brothers of Dewsbury perhaps deserve first mention.

Mark Newsome, junior, and his brother, Alf, were both established in business by their father, a former Lord Mayor of Dewsbury. Mark managed the firm of Newsome, Sons, and Spedding, rug and blanket manufacturers, of Aldams Mill, whilst Alf, an engineer by trade, ran the Anchor Foundry. As Dewsbury, and the blanket factory, in particular, became something of a magnet for several Welshmen following Dewsbury's Welsh tours in the mid-1880s, it is perhaps not that surprising to find that Mark Newsome - who denied ever paying players for their rugby services - seconded the proposal for broken-time in 1893. More surprising, perhaps, is the fact that he played no part in the formation of the Northern Union. This was left to other industrialists and entrepreneurs, who claimed that they were equally as determined as Newsome to see that professionalism was not introduced into rugby, either in 1893 or 1895.

As both the Newsomes' playing careers are synonymous with the Yorkshire Cup, and the dispute which would indirectly bring *"veiled professionalism"* out into the open, we perhaps need only mention at this stage that Alf was famous for his hand-off, and was nicknamed *"The Man in White"* after once forgetting his kit and being loaned a Yorkshire county jersey; and that both players retired in their early twenties, after the Yorkshire Cup dispute in 1883. Mark, however, later took up refereeing and was a leading official during the period in question.

Not only would the Yorkshire Cup raise the issue of *"veiled professionalism"* but it would ultimately threaten the southerners' hold on the balance of power, and bring about the prospect of the legalisation of broken-time payments.

Although the Hospital Cup dates from 1874, the Rugby Union fought shy of introducing a national cup competition to rival the F. A. Cup; in 1875/6 they refused to accept the gift of a trophy valued at over £150 from the Royal Military Academy, Woolwich, and in 1880/1 a similar proposal was also left on the table.

Spurred by the success of the F. A. Cup and the Sheffield Association Cup, however, the Yorkshire Rugby Union were not so reticent. It was

Arthur E. Hudson (a member of the Leeds merchants and manufacturers, Hudson, Sykes, & Bousfield) in conjunction with Bradford club members, H. W. T. Garnett, a paper manufacturer, and F. Schutt, a partner in H. Schutt & Co., yarn merchants, who proposed the Yorkshire Challenge Cup *("T'Owd Tin Pot")*. Played in successive weeks throughout December, 1877, entry was limited to the following sixteen clubs centred around the main worsted and mining centres of the West Riding: Bradford, Bradford Caledonians, Bradford Zingari, Bradford Juniors, Halifax, Huddersfield, Leeds St. John's, Leeds, Kirkstall, Wakefield, Wakefield Trinity, Dewsbury, Heckmondwike, and Mirfield - together with York and Hull from the East Riding.

The chief interest centred on the semi-final at Apperley Bridge, Bradford, which decided the vexed question of whether the self-taught working-class players of Halifax, *"....most of whom had barely three years experience of the game, could match men who had played the game since school-days."* Although one ex-player was unable to make the journey from Ceylon, Bradford managed to obtain the services of players from as far afield as Dublin (Fred Schutt), Derby and Liverpool. It was to no avail, however, and the home-spun Halifax side went all the way to that first final in which they defeated York on the Holbeck Recreation ground, the game having been switched on the morning of the match from Huddersfield due to the Rifle Field being waterlogged.

From attendances it is possible to estimate the immense interest which surrounded this competition. A good cup run, however, did not necessarily guarantee that a club would benefit financially, as all the profits in the finals and the semi-finals went to local charities. Furthermore, most of the leading clubs were opposed to the introduction of shared-gates with junior clubs, preferring to risk the outcome of the draw in order to benefit from their greater support, which later compelled them to enclose their grounds and make substantial improvements to their facilities.

The debts which accrued from such enterprises were later to prove a major factor prior to the split and in the Northern Union's formative years. On 2 April, 1892, however, Leeds could rejoice that they had hit the jackpot, when a crowd of 27,654 - a figure which exceeded the F.A. Cup Final the previous season, and the highest ever in the north for a rugby union game prior to the split - packed into the recently-opened Headingley for the third round tie against Halifax.

A description of the scene at a game between Bradford and Wakefield Trinity at Park Avenue in 1884 would indicate that rugby at that time enjoyed the support of all classes of the population:

*...in the presence of that vast crowd - four walls of human faces, all seemingly*

*inspired by the same spirit of enthusiasm....Had not Bradford sent thither its foremost citizens? Was not every rung on the social ladder there represented, from the highest to the lowest? The church, the law, medicine, trade, industry, idleness, wealth, poverty, beauty, ugliness - all had their prominent representatives.*

And correspondence, following the 1891 Yorkshire Cup Final, would also appear to indicate that, off the field, this middle-class interest (although decidedly lukewarm in the case of the writer) had been maintained:

*I too was a unit of the many thousands that attended the match at Headingley on Saturday - the final Cup-tie, in fact, being my sole annual football treat. The game must indeed be coming more popular than ever, for in my immediate vicinity (on the uncovered stand) I was surprised, and agreeably so, to notice doctors, lawyers, parsons, and even the magistracy swelling the immense crowd by their presence....*[17]

From this casual follower's incredulity one can naturally assume that in those days rugby was a game of the masses, and this appears to be true, not only in Lancashire and Yorkshire, but in other parts of the north. It remains open to conjecture, however, as to whether or not large sections of the middle-classes gradually dissociated themselves from rugby in the north, with the advent of the Northern Union and the legitimization of payments to players.

In contrast to the above, a Yorkshire reporter, at the Middlesex-Yorkshire match in February, 1893, commented that:

*The followers of the game in the south are evidently "swells" and the writer has certainly never seen as many top hats at a score of matches in the north as he saw at Richmond on this one day.*

Allowing for northern prejudice, and the fact that this game was played on Monday afternoon, when working men may well have been otherwise engaged, it does suggest that the social backgrounds of supporters in the London area may well have mirrored those of the southern players.

What is more certain is the likelihood that in the capital there could have been few, if any, scenes to match the after-match celebrations which awaited the victorious Tudhoe side on their home-coming after beating Hartlepool Rovers in the 1892 Durham Senior Cup. They epitomised the close community spirit which was aroused by the various cup competitions in the north - competitions which were either rejected totally, or were slow to be adopted by the southern traditionalists:

*On Saturday night the arrival of the excursion train from Sunderland to Spennymoor containing the Tudhoe team and some 800 admirers streamed into the station about 9.30 p.m., where a brake and three horses, the Whitworth brass band, and some 10,000 people were assembled to give the heroes a reception, which was of a most enthusiastic character, so enthusiastic indeed was the crowd that the horses were taken out of the brake, and the team were drawn by the members of the second and third teams, preceded by the band playing "The Conquering Hero" ...At the club headquarters, the North-Eastern Hotel, the large room was packed to suffocation to inspect the cup, which was over and over again filled.*[18]

The above cup had been contested first in 1880, the same year that Cheshire and Northumberland inaugurated their trophy, whilst the Midland Counties (1881/2) and Cumberland in 1882 quickly followed suit. Lancashire, however, steadfastly refused to sanction a county-wide Cup - a proposal in 1886 by Werneth having been defeated - leaving the sub-unions of South-East Lancashire (formed 1877) and West Lancashire (formed 1884) to run their own highly successful cups.

In the north the introduction of other local charity cup competitions, some of which still survive under rugby league auspices, also encouraged an allegiance to one particular sport and the finals generated the same amount of rejoicing in the smaller hamlets and districts as the county cups. In 1884, for example, the Bradford Charity Cup, which was presented by the Mayor, Alderman Isaac Smith, and the Holliday Cup in Huddersfield were both inaugurated; and for 1885/6 the Halifax (Infirmary) Charity Challenge Cup, which was originally valued at 50 guineas and donated by Mr Shaw, M.P., was promoted by the Halifax and Friendly Trade Society. Reverend Marshall refereed the 1885 Bradford Charity Cup final at Bradford's Park Avenue, which was watched by a crowd of 8-10,000. Fred Richmond won this match for Manningham, against Cleckheaton, with a last-minute drop kick, which Frank Marshall later measured as having travelled (presumably to the point at which it landed) 70 yards. Just how popular derby competitions were can be judged by the fact that the final of the Wigan Union Charity Challenge Cup between Wigan and Aspull on 24 April, 1886 drew 15-18,000 to Dicconson Street - a crowd which far exceeded those at internationals held at Blackheath's Rectory Field.

It was 1890 before the southerners realised the benefits of knock-out competitions, with Bristol, Kent, Eastern Counties, Hampshire, and Northants, all introducing cups around this time. It was not until March, 1893, however, that Surrey decided to institute a Challenge Cup, but by this time most of the bigger London clubs were standing down from such competitions, and there was an apathetic response in 1894 for a Middlesex Cup, with the latter scheme being abandoned due to only seven entries being received, partly due to the Union itself being divided on the issue. The reason for this southern reluctance was perhaps summed up by the Kent secretary, Rowland Hill, who had originally supported the proposal for a cup in his own county:

*The competition in Kent had been introduced as a last resource, in the hope of stopping the game from dying out in certain parts of the county. Cup competitions have undoubtedly created a large amount of interest, and if, after they had given a genuine impetus, they could be dropped, good rather than evil might have resulted from them, but in some districts the system has been permitted to assume large proportions and it is responsible for many evils which have crept into the game, notably betting, which is an unmitigated curse to any branch of athletics which it contaminates.*[19]

He was referring here, of course, to matters in the north, where early experiences had rightly given the southerners cause for concern. Cheshire, for example, had passed a resolution in April, 1881, *"That the cup-ties be discontinued as detrimental to the best interests of the game in the county, and tending to promote bad feeling"*. Following the 1883/4 Durham Cup final between Hartlepool Rovers and North Durham, a resolution to withdraw the senior cup was defeated by only one vote. For 1885/6 the Durham committee actually succeeded in having it withdrawn, only for it to be reinstated in 1886 after pressure from the clubs.

The Yorkshire Cup also came under threat of withdrawal with even Hudson, the original promoter of the scheme, as early as 1881, regretting the course that he had helped set in motion. His own club, Yorkshire Wanderers - *"The only genteel club in Yorkshire"*, as it was christened by one scribe - which he had formed in an attempt to emulate the exclusiveness of Manchester, withdrew from the Yorkshire Cup in 1881/2 on the grounds that such games were too rough and unsporting; and Halifax also refused to enter that same year, apparently because some of the players had been told that *"betting men"* had offered rewards to the other teams to lame them. Bradford's subsequent refusal to compete in 1888 and 1889 was merely delayed by the rule change in July, 1886, whereby attacks on referees were punishable by clubs having their entry cancelled or being drawn away from home.

Despite its problems, however, the Yorkshire Cup continued to attract increasing numbers of entries. Writing in his school magazine in February, 1889, Reverend Marshall had this to say about the effects which the Challenge Cup had brought to the game and the relative strength of Yorkshire rugby, not only with the south, but with Lancashire:

*The fact is that the growing popularity of the game...has engendered a spirit of rivalry and keenness to win that has led players and clubs to think more of the success of the day than of the character of the play that has been exhibited....there is hardly a village in the West Riding of Yorkshire that has not a football club, and the usual amount of enthusiastic followers ready to extol the team generally and the prominent members thereof in particular.*

33

*It is these followers that have done the great harm to football as regards the class of game to be played...To win the Cup is the one aim and intent of the prominent clubs....And what have been the results of the Cup competition? Its evils have been many and pronounced. A style of game deserving of the severest reprobation - rough play, off-side play, lying on the ball, the development of wing forwards - the readiness to find any excuse whereby a defeated team may appeal to the county committee to obtain a reversal of the decision of the game.*

Marshall had to concede, however, that the Yorkshire Challenge Cup had *"more than counterbalanced these evils"* and had directly resulted in making Yorkshire by far the strongest county in the country. *"Eliminate Blackheath, Richmond, London Scottish, and perhaps the Old Leysians from the London clubs,"* he wrote, *"and what chance would any of the remainder have with what are perhaps considered the second flight of Yorkshire clubs."* As the question was entirely rhetorical Marshall did not even bother to add the question mark.

This marked superiority was also confirmed in an article in 1892 by *"Londoner"*:

*If we take the play of the northern clubs as a standard I am afraid that we have to confess that our average of play is an uncommonly low one - in fact Blackheath and the London Scottish were the only Metropolitan 15s last season who could compete with a crack northern 15 with any hope of success.... The majority of Yorkshire fifteens are composed of working men, who have only adopted football in recent years, and have received no school education in the art. The majority of the members of the London clubs have played it all their lives, yet when the two meet there is only one in it - the Yorkshiremen. How is it, then, that the latter, despite his want of school tuition in the game can beat the former, who has learnt it with his Latin grammar? The only reason I can assign is a want of keenness, a want of condition, a want of pride in the record of one's club, and a want of energetic club management.*[20]

This casual approach to the game in the south is reflected generally in the later start to the season, and the smaller number of fixtures, vis a vis the northern clubs. The restriction of the close-season from 1889 was aimed really at the north, as southern clubs were not accustomed to starting until the second or third week in September. In 1893/4, for example, although Old Leysians played 30 games, Blackheath played only 25 and started their season on 30 September, 1893; whilst Queens 22, Harlequins 21, Marlborough Nomads 19 and Richmond 19 each, Guys 18, and London Scottish 17 played even less. In contrast, many Yorkshire and Lancashire clubs played over 40 games (West Riding managed to squeeze in 51) and started their season on 2 September.

There was also a different emphasis placed on pre-match preparation. Whilst the southerners considered any form of training to be opposed to the traditions and etiquette of public school *"style"*, northern clubs, particularly when the cup ties came round, had, what was then considered to be, a more *"professional"* approach - although this was perhaps laughable by today's standards. This generally appears to have taken the form of free binges, and the employment, in some cases, of professional trainers to help wear off this over-indulgence. Following the 1886 professional regulations, a Yorkshire newspaper remarked:

*The blow which deprives the average footballer of his steaks and ale, legs of mutton, port wine etc, during the cup ties will be severely felt. The Rugby Union...have a strong objection against training for football, contending that if a player abstains from foolish excesses and takes moderate exercise he will always been in condition. This, no doubt is true enough, but the indulgence in the "extras" during the ties has prevailed so long in the West Riding that they are looked upon as an institution, and their prohibition will create some soreness. There is no doubt, though, that their maintenance is inconsistent with the principle of amateurism.*

Batley's trainer and baggage-man, ex-miner Richard Webster (*"London Dick"*), who was apparently *"the first man to bring forth a Yorkshire Cup winning team"* - against Manningham in 1885 - had his own elixir which he also shared with visiting teams. In 1886 neighbours Dewsbury appointed Tommy Conlon, *"the antediluvian and whilom professional long distance runner."* What was an accepted practice in the north, however, was frowned on by southern players and officials.

During the after dinner speech which followed England's defeat of Ireland in Dublin 1886, Dr Arthur *"Jimmy"* Budd, the Blackheath and England forward, had warned the Bradford internationals (Robertshaw, Bonsor, and Wilkinson) of the dangers of overtraining, *"which he feared was much practiced in Yorkshire"*. In March 1892, however, Bradford were said to be in strict training and practicing two nights a week, with an additional players' meeting on the Friday night before games. At the same time, one Bradford forward had also been dropped as a disciplinary measure. This was a clear indication that the relationship between clubs and players in the north, particularly following the introduction of leagues the following season, was on a different standing to that in the south.

Northerners also had the advantage, from that first Roses match in 1871, of having provided each other with keen competition at county level, Yorkshire, Lancashire, Cheshire, Northumberland and Durham, having kept up a series of unbroken matches. Nowhere was the rivalry as pronounced as that between Lancashire and Yorkshire: from 1871 until 1881 Yorkshire had beaten Lancashire only once, but from 1882 onwards Lancashire recorded only one victory, and that, in 1884, was when the strong Bradford contingent were on their southern tour. The following sample of attendances and gate receipts will give some idea of the popularity of these contests: 1887 Yorkshire v. Lancashire at Bradford £380; 1888 Lancashire v. Yorkshire at Whalley Range *"Over £400 and Manchester races took £100 away;"* 1889 Yorkshire v. Lancashire at Bradford 14,515 (£591); 1891 Yorkshire v. Lancashire at Huddersfield 23,270 (£830); and 1892 Lancashire v. Yorkshire at Fallowfield 15,000.

By comparison to the above figures the £110 gate for the Somerset versus Maoris encounter in 1891 was described as *"the largest ever in the West"*; and, on a Wednesday afternoon in December of that year, a crowd estimated at only 600 were at Blackheath for the Kent-Middlesex match. Discussing the prospects of legalising full professionalism (not broken-time) in rugby in 1892, one commentator confirmed this general lack of public support for the game south of the River Trent by stating:

*The Southerners do not like (professionalism) because it cannot help them to any extent. They don't get the gate money, nor yet the support, which would enable their clubs to keep paid talent. Neither would such talent mix at all well with the home product.*[21]

Indeed, it would appear from the situation described by Hartlepool Rovers' international three-quarter, F. H. R. Alderson, a Cambridge blue who played for Blackheath whilst at University, that the southern clubs found it difficult to even manage paying expenses:

*The management was far ahead of anything I had seen in the South. No trouble about tickets or hotels, everything was arranged for you. You had simply to walk to the station and get in the saloon....It was a change to me after scrambling about for a ticket at Cannon Street every time I went to the Rectory Field at Blackheath.*[22]

Because of the negligible amount of gate money in the south, in the very early days, northern counties had subsidised the southern counties in order to enable them to fulfil their fixtures. Devon, Somerset, Gloucester and the Midlands were said to be more enthusiastic over county rugby than the London counties, but, nonetheless, when Yorkshire beat Midland Counties at Wakefield in 1882/3 the visitors played a man short (because of a dispute Moseley, the leading club, had refused to assist the county), whilst in the return the Midlanders' lack of post-match hospitality was accounted for by the fact that they were short of funds. Although Middlesex were unquestionably the leading county in 1887/8 when Somerset also beat Yorkshire, southern apathy generally for such games was epitomised in 1889 with the *"fiasco"*, as their secretary, Rowland Hill, called it, of Kent not being able to raise a team for their game against Yorkshire.

This was not to say that the southerners took kindly to what was termed "*northern cockiness*". This is well illustrated by the fact that Middlesex invariably included players who appeared not to have the necessary county qualifications, even though eligibility rules had been introduced in 1883/4. When Yorkshire lost to Stoddart's drop goal in 1886 (only goals counting in those days) even though they had scored three tries without reply, the Middlesex team was described as a "*Scoto-English or Middlesex-cum-Kent-Surrey and Oxford Fifteen, or whatever you choose to call it.*"

R. E. Lockwood, Yorkshire's captain for the game against Middlesex on 30 January, 1893, also had this to say, later in his career:

*There was always a strong feeling against us in the south, not of bitterness, but a consuming desire to "take the stuffing out of us". For instance, there was that famous team that Middlesex got together to beat us at Richmond in which Scotland, Wales and the rest of England got submerged by some wonderful process.*

*There were three international captains - A. E. Stoddart (England), R. G. MacMillan (Scotland) and A. J. Gould (Wales); and Lord knows how many more famous men all brought together to take the starch out of Yorkshire. Sammy Woods came into our dressing rooms before the commencement of the game and asked if we thought we should win this time. "It isn't a case of winning", I said in chaff, "but we've been considering how high to pile the score." We simply ran away with them as you know".*[23]

Prior to 1890, the Rugby Union had declared the county champions based on national results, but in that year Yorkshire's scheme was passed, which split the country into four districts - much of the credit for its ingenuity being given to Reverend Marshall. From the inauguration of this official county championship until the split in 1895, Yorkshire took the title on six of the seven occasions, losing only three of 55 games, with Lancashire winning in 1891. On many occasions Yorkshire were able to select younger players without any effect on the side's performance, and such was the talent available in Yorkshire that, even after the break-away of the leading clubs, they still managed to field a championship-winning side which was the equal of any that had gone before.

There is evidence that prior to 1895 most of the Rugby Union's wealth was a result of the popularity of the game in the north. All of England's early internationals were played at the Oval before crowds of 3-4,000, and it was not until England met Scotland at Manchester's Whalley Range on 28 February, 1880 that the Rugby Union began to benefit substantially from the fixture. This game produced a profit exceeding £250 after gifts to charities. Crowds for internationals at Blackheath's Rectory Field did not match those at ordinary fixtures in the north, with the 12,000 at the game against the Maoris being near to its capacity. The first international in Yorkshire was on 5 January, 1884 when England played Wales at Cardigan Fields, Leeds, before a disappointing 3,000, but for the next international in the city, at Headingley on 4 March, 1893, a crowd of 19,583 (including Leeds members), plus 2,000 reserved and complimentary ticket holders, produced receipts of £1,356.

Because of the international dispute, and the loss of finance from this source, the Rugby Union also re-introduced the North versus South fixture and the champion county versus the Rest of England, which again proved highly lucrative due to Yorkshire and Lancashire's involvement. For example, 1890 Yorkshire v. England at Bradford £402; 1891 Lancashire v. England at Whalley Range (£700 went to charities); and 1892 Yorkshire v Rest of England at Leeds 20,479 (£1,075).

The fact that most of the Rugby Union's funds had come from games which had been staged in the north would be referred to by Joe Platt, the first secretary of the Northern Union, at that body's 1897 AGM:

*A "Budd" in the south had told them they would never get into flower and that they could not afford to leave a Union which had £3,000 invested in Consuls. It was not £3,000 they wanted but justice; and they could not get it. As a matter of fact they all knew that a greater proportion of that money had come out of the north of England."*

If Joe Platt included in his *"justice"* the need for proportional representation on the national committee, and the need for general meetings to be held in the north, then that part of the country certainly appears to have suffered an injustice prior to 1895.

The Rugby Union's membership had expanded from 31 clubs in 1871/2 to 59 for the following season, but, although in 1873/4 there were some 104 adult clubs in England, by 1877/8 there were still only 26 clubs from the whole of the north in membership. Both Manchester and Liverpool were rewarded with seats on the committee as early as 1874, but at the time that J. MacLaren (Manchester) was elected as the north's first Rugby Union President in 1882, the Yorkshire press was airing their complaints over the large number of southerners on the committee, and the inconvenience and inequitable arrangement of holding all meetings in London.

*Not a single Yorkshireman attended the October meeting of the Rugby Union...an indication that after past experiences the Tykes were not prepared to undertake a long journey for the mere purpose of participating in a gathering almost solely composed of Southerners, and whose deliberations were only an hour's duration.....As regards the officers elected for the present year, it cannot fairly be said that the choice will find much favour in the eyes of the northerners in general, since out of twenty seats only seven have been allocated to gentlemen connected with the northern clubs - a very unfair representation to say the least, and quite in keeping with the past traditions and monopoly held by the southern contingent.*

To emphasise the point, the same leader also referred to the fact that the West Kent-Blackheath game was simply abandoned after the home side were further reduced through injuries after only being able to raise thirteen men:

> *The apathy of the southern players is proverbial, yet in the face of such a fact they retain London as the headquarters of the Union, fill its coffers in the north, and are once more in possession of great voting preponderance on the board!* [24]

And this situation would continue despite the remarkable growth of the game in the north. Following Yorkshire's introduction in 1887 of an increased subscription of £1½ gns, which entitled clubs, not only to membership of the county and the Challenge Cup, but to full membership of the Rugby Union, the number of clubs in that county greatly increased. Alarmed at this threat, at the 1890 AGM, when Yorkshire's Harry Garnett retired from the Rugby Union Presidency, the committee proposed that only three seats of the 17-man committee should be allocated to Yorkshire. Moreover, it took all the persuasive powers of James Miller to gain their entitlement to a fourth seat on the board, Reverend Marshall taking the place of the proposed Devon representative. By the time of the broken-time meeting in 1893, however, Yorkshire, with close on a third of all the clubs affiliated to the Rugby Union, were certainly entitled to additional representation.

It was not this committee representation, of course, which would decide the outcome of the Yorkshire proposal for broken-time in 1893, but the voting strength of clubs at the general meeting. An estimated breakdown of the membership of the various northern counties would indicate that about 250 of the Rugby Union's 481 clubs and unions at that time came from north of the River Trent. This is made up as follows: Yorkshire 150, Lancashire 35, Cumberland 26, Durham 18, Cheshire 9, Northumberland 9, Westmoreland 4. This northern figure, may have been much higher, as the Rugby Union's membership had risen sharply from 388 in 1892, and at that time 150 of those clubs already came from Yorkshire. It should not be assumed, however, that many of these additional one hundred clubs would also have come from Yorkshire, as entry to the Yorkshire Cup at this time was already limited to 132. Lancashire's total was much less than Yorkshire's, due to the fact that, with no county-wide cup competition, there was less compulsion for clubs to join either the county or the national unions. Overall, however, bearing in mind the southerners' past apathy, there were possibly sufficient votes in the north to achieve a two-thirds majority.

But just how accurate is this assumption of a north-south divide, specifically as to how it affected the voting in 1893? Firstly, such a *"Two Nations"* assessment clearly fails to take account of the differing backgrounds, viewpoints, and personal aspirations of key northern officials, some of whom tended to represent themselves rather than public opinion. Principally, however, it fails to consider the position of the northern working-class junior clubs - one commentator went so far as to call them, *"Tin-pot organisation(s) with a guinea, a ball, and a pair of goal posts"* - many of which were as opposed, as any southern club, to the prospect of broken-time being introduced. Unlike the southerners, however, such clubs, particularly in Lancashire and Yorkshire, had to face the loss of their best players to the neighbouring gate-taking clubs.

Even if they agreed with the justice theory of broken-time, few, if any, junior clubs were able to afford it. The question that must really be asked, therefore, is why any junior club should have gone to the expense of travelling to London in order to support such a proposal? The answer, of course, must lie in the fact that they may have considered broken-time to be in their own self-interest, chiefly based on the argument, put forward by its proponents, that broken-time was a barrier to the greater threat of full professionalism. Some junior clubs also needed to pacify their senior neighbours, on whom they relied for financial support through the playing of annual testimonial games. Having said that, however, not every Yorkshire junior club delegate, who attended the broken-time meeting, would vote in favour of their own committee's proposal.

The north-south theory is further flawed in the respect that the four most northern counties were subjected to the loss of players to Lancashire and Yorkshire, although, in the case of West Hartlepool, it was certainly not one-way traffic along the east coast. Such as Kendal Hornets, however, appear to have been particularly badly hit by these southerly migrations - for example, six of their former players were in the St. Helens side which faced them in March, 1889, and they later lost seven of their 9-a-side championship team to Tyldesley, St. Helens, Leigh, and Bradford. Understandably, therefore, Yorkshire's broken-time proposal would find few sympathisers among the Cumberland, Westmoreland, Durham and Northumberland clubs - nor, it seems with clubs in Cheshire. Furthermore, far from acting in unison, the animosity between Lancashire and Yorkshire rugby was said to be legendary.

Yorkshire correspondents referred to Lancashire's *"spitefulness"* on account of Yorkshire's County Championship successes, Reverend Marshall's intervention in the Oldham business and also of the pact which southerners and Lancastrians had on the national committee -

Liverpool and Manchester, particularly, having been closely identified with the southern public school elite from the early days of the Rugby Union. At the AGM on 4 October, 1888, for example, J. H. Payne (Lancashire) supported the Rugby Union committee recommendation that William Cail (Northumberland) should be placed on the list of Senior Vice-Presidents, who by rotation were appointed to the highest office in the game. This was in direct opposition to Yorkshire's nomination of Harry Garnett, who, they argued, deserved to fill the vacancy of George Thomson, who had died on his arrival in Australia. The large Yorkshire delegation, on this occasion, helped get Garnett elected, but in 1891 they were not so successful.

Following that Rugby Union AGM on 16 September, when a majority of clubs (143-106) voted in favour of Yorkshire's proposal to hold general meetings alternately in the north and south, but the reform failed to get the necessary two-thirds majority, an editor in that county had this say:

*A confident belief prevails that a determined attack will be made upon the Board, and an endeavour made to capture several of the seats at present held by Lancashire and the south....We have sufficient votes to snap and break the tyrannous authority which Southerner and Lancastrian now relentlessly exercise over holding all meetings in the metropolis....*[25]

The vote at Lancashire's AGM had been 19-15 against the Yorkshire proposal, and F. A. Grover (Swinton) had argued that, *"The meetings, if held in the north, would fall under the exclusive control of Yorkshire, who were drawing a red herring across the path, and were trying to make the Rugby Union an accessory of Yorkshire."* Furthermore, a list of Lancashire clubs and Rugby Union committee members from that county, who were said to have voted against Yorkshire at the Rugby Union's AGM, showed that these included not only the counties of Northumberland, Cumberland, Cheshire, Durham, and Lancashire, but the following northern clubs: Oldham, Salford, Swinton, Millom, Broughton Rangers, Broughton, St. Helens Recs, Runcorn, Birkenhead, Rockcliff, Northern, the Northumberland club, and Wigan. Almondbury Grammar School were said to have been the only Yorkshire club to have voted against![26]

What is more important than that single vote, however, is the fact that Reverend Marshall unintentionally averted Yorkshire's possible control of the game, if we are to believe *The Yorkshireman* which said that:

*The Lancashire representatives voted against it out of sheer spite; a mean return for the unofficial action of a Yorkshireman in regard to the Oldham club last season. That's the truth of the matter, put bluntly.*

This was, in many ways, a more crucial vote than the broken-time meeting in 1893, as it was feared that by taking meetings away from

41

London the Rugby Union would lose its representative character and that decision-making would fall into the hands of the most powerful section. One could argue, therefore, that several present leading rugby league clubs, by being instrumental in voting for the *status quo* in 1891, also helped stave off the possibility that the Rugby Union would be governed from the north, under the control of the county which most favoured broken-time - a proposal which Lancashire clubs generally would, only half-heartedly, support.

Far from it being a case of a north-south divide, therefore, it might be considered that it was really a matter of Yorkshire versus the Rest.

# Chapter Three
# Professionalism in other Sports

As rugby did not exist in a vacuum, it is impossible to fully understand the varying attitudes towards the issue of paying players in the 1880s and 1890s without reference to other sports. Before, therefore, we examine the nature and extent of *"professionalism"* in rugby during this period we need to have a wider historical perspective of such events. In so doing, it should soon become apparent that the various definitions of what constituted an *"amateur"* or *"professional"* were not only extremely arbitrary but were usually related to a player's social status rather than the fact that he might be paid for his services. Many *"amateur"* cricketers, and a few *"amateur"* footballers, for example, earned more than their professional counterparts.

Several northern critics argued that these same double-standards also applied to the gentlemen amateurs from the southern rugby clubs and Universities when they availed themselves of the lavish hospitality of their northern hosts. However, the need for a clamp-down on the excesses of this privileged section of society was clearly not in the minds of the Rugby Union sub-committee which drafted the first professional regulations in 1886. Significantly these were introduced only a year after professionalism was legalised in soccer, from which the term *"broken-time"* first originated.

Professional sport, however, usually under the patronage of the aristocracy, dates from the 18th century. Before the 1850s and the emergence of the Victorian amateur ethos with its moral overtones there was no social stigma attached to making money out of sport, gambling and prize money being an integral part of the enjoyment.

Horse racing and boxing spring most readily to mind in this category but it is cricket which is of particular relevance to our study, in that many of their mercenary traits were inherited by both football codes; and for a fair number of multi-talented rugby players there was a good living to be made during the summer months as professional cricketers at local league and county level.

The first rules of cricket were drawn up by the Duke of Richmond in

1727 primarily for the purpose of regulating the country house games on which large wagers were usually laid. The M.C.C. was formed in 1787 and took over from the Hambleton Club as the game's governing body. Apart from joining the staff of Lords or the Oval, in the 1840s there were only three opportunities for a cricketer to make a living from the game: he could seek employment from a wealthy patron, become a practice bowler at university or public school, or bowl for one of the elite local clubs. The formation by William Clarke in 1846 of the All England XI not only provided work for a troupe of touring professionals (they were paid the then princely sum of £5 per match) but it popularised the game nationally and was the catalyst for the establishment of similar peripatetic sides. Although Nottingham, was, according to Sissons, *"for many decades the epicentre of professional cricket"*, the All England XI's first game on 31 August, 1846, took place in Hyde Park, Sheffield against 20 of that city. Despite the great stimulus which Clarke's enterprise gave for the employment of cricket professionals there were still only 110 listed in Fred Lillywhite's Guide of 1854.[1]

By the mid-1860s there was a concerted campaign, orchestrated principally by James Pycroft, editor of *The Cricket Field*, to undermine the influence of the professionals. He argued that it would be, *"prejudicial to the game to grow too professional"*, and, *"a mistake to allow professionals to extensively take the place of amateurs in the great matches"*. From 1873 the M.C.C. and the counties effectively reduced the professionals' mobility and their earning power by introducing a 2-year residential rule and a stipulation that a cricketer could represent only one county. Sadly, because of such restrictions many of the early professionals became destitute in their old age and several committed suicide through despair.

In contrast the earnings of the *"veiled professionals"* who posed as simon pure gentleman amateurs were ignored by the establishment. Sissons cites many cases where the M.C.C's definition of an amateur, *"that no gentlemen ought to make a profit from his services on the cricket field"*, was patently abused. The most famous example of this social paradox is, of course, Dr. W. G. Grace, who is estimated to have made over £120,000 from cricket, being paid ten times the professionals pay for the 1873/4 tour to Australia and receiving two testimonials totalling over £10,000, whilst retaining his amateur status. It is perhaps worth reflecting that as the second of these testimonials was being launched during the summer of 1895, which finally made Grace richer by almost £9,000, the rugby fraternity was in a state of turmoil, ostensibly over the refusal to legitimise broken-time payments of only a few shillings a day to the working man.

The *"veiled professionalism"* in cricket was a creation of the pressures on the middle-class cricketer who had insufficient financial means to play as a true amateur, but who, nonetheless, would not accept the social stigma attached to being a professional.

The distinction between the amateur Gentleman and the professional Player, a situation which survived until 1962, could hardly have been improved on had it been devised by the South African apartheid regime. As with all Victorian employees the professional cricketer was constantly reminded of his lower social status. Segregation from his amateur colleagues took many forms and included the use of separate dressing rooms and entrances onto the field of play, discriminatory travel and hotel arrangements, and, where professionals were invited into the tea room, they sat at their own tables and had different menus. They had to address the amateur as Mr or Sir and they were subjected to strict discipline from the county committees.

From the 1880s it was accepted that only amateurs could captain their counties. Lord Hawkes's famous, and apparently misunderstood, plea in 1925, *"Pray God, no professional will ever captain England"*, appeared to epitomise this situation. When, in an emergency, Jack Hobbs took over the captaincy during the fourth test against Australia at Old Trafford in 1926 he became the first professional to do so since Arthur Shrewsbury in 1877.

Shrewsbury had played for the All England XI in the mid-1870s and together with Alfred Shaw was one of the seven Nottinghamshire professionals who threatened to strike after asking for £20 for the 1880 Australian tour game. As partners in a sports goods firm they organised three cricket tours to Australia and the first ever rugby tour from these shores in 1888. As open professionals and entrepreneurs they were, of course, motivated by profit, but that they did not always succeed was due, in part, to the so-called amateur cricketers' inflated expenses.[2]

One such amateur was the double international and captain of England at both cricket and rugby, and playing partner of Shrewsbury, Andrew Ernest Stoddart.[3] Born in South Shields in 1863, Stoddart became the darling of the Lords' and Blackheath crowds, for his stylish batting and three-quarter play, respectively. John Darling, Australia's captain who toured England between 1896 and 1905, however, cited him as one of the highly paid professionals who operated under the guise of an amateur during his period in the game. At the time of the 1896 England strike George Lohmann, one of five professionals who demanded increased fees, had condemned the fact that the amateurs were receiving in expenses twice the amount being offered to the professionals. Attention in the press to Grace and Stoddart's inflated expenses resulted in the latter withdrawing from the test. A member of the Stock Exchange and later secretary of the Queens Club, Andrew Stoddart committed suicide in 1915 whilst of unsound mind due to losing all his money as a result of the outbreak of the First World War. There is now strong evidence to suggest that *"The Prince of Centres"*, as he was known, was paid by Shrewsbury for his services whilst on the above rugby tour, which extended the time he had been away from his business to 14 months, having been recruited whilst out with George Frederic Vernon's side in Australia.

A barrister by profession, Vernon had represented England against Australia in 1882 whilst an amateur cricketer with Middlesex, and was engaged by the Melbourne Club to sign up players for the 1887/8 tour. An Old Rugbeian and Blackheath and Middlesex line out expert, who finished his days on the Gold Coast of Australia, Vernon made the first of his five appearances for England in the first international to be staged at Lansdowne Road in 1878, when he partnered the celebrated Lancashire sportsman, Old Harrovanian Albert Neilson Hornby.

*"Monkey"* Hornby was the first player to captain England concurrently at both rugby and cricket. His inherited wealth - his father had been a cotton manufacturer and the first Lord Mayor of Blackburn - and his marriage to the daughter of the publisher of the *London Illustrated News*, enabled Hornby to live the life of a country squire and devote his time to his many sporting interests, which naturally included hunting and other field sports. *"Monkey"* - a nickname inherited at Harrow from his brother - declined to play in the North versus South rugby match in 1883 as it would have interfered with his plans for a shooting week-end. Regarded as, *"The Father of Football in Blackburn"*, having formed a club under Harrow Rules before the famous Blackburn Olympic and Rovers, he captained Lancashire at cricket for twenty of the years from 1867-1899 and, representing Preston Grasshoppers and Manchester, was a rugby international from 1877-1882. The game against Scotland in 1882 marked not only the retirement of Hornby from international rugby, but it was also the occasion for another important Lancashire sportsman to make his international debut.[4]

John Henry Payne, a solicitor, educated at Manchester Grammar School, Cheltenham College, and St. John's College, Cambridge, was an extremely skilful half-back, who captained Lancashire for many years. A stumper and middle-order batsman, he played nine matches for Lancashire in 1883 as an amateur, after making his first-class debut for Cambridge University against an England XI in 1880. Payne was joint secretary and treasurer of the Lancashire Rugby Union, as well as being a Lancashire representative on the Rugby Union committee, at the time of the broken-time conflict.[5]

On this issue, Payne and Hornby did not see eye to eye, whilst the latter, whilst unexpectedly promoting the cause of broken-time in rugby, was also prepared to raise the question of the hypocrisy of the supposedly amateur sportsman. Alongside such *"shamateurs"*, who Hornby exposed, there are a few cases during this period of rugby players playing professionally with their counties and earning an honest living. J. T. Brown, the Driffield rugby captain, in 1893, and stumper Arthur *"Sandy"* Bairstow (see below), both represented Yorkshire, for example. For most working-class players, however, it was the money made in the numerous local cricket leagues which was their main source of summer income - local league cricket being so popular with the public in Yorkshire and Lancashire that it threatened the viability of the county championship. Most major league sides employed professionals, who were usually also found employment as groundsmen.

Just a few examples are listed of what was a widespread practice among rugby players in the 1880 and 1890s, with players being prepared to travel south or to Scotland to find work. Hull's vice-captain, Herbert Bell, was professional with Goole in 1887; Harry Noble played for Heckmondwike C.C., but was due to move south where he was to be the professional for one of the military college schools; Herbert Hartley (Brighouse Rangers) kept wicket all summer for Brighouse after being suspended at rugby; in 1890 Wakefield Trinity's *"Teddy"* Bartram and Harry Hayley were professionals with North Leeds, whilst the former signed a sixteen week engagement with Newcastle for the following season; and, finally, after a professional engagement with Failsworth, Bradford's Willie Jowett joined Crichton (Dumfries) for 1892.

It was partly in deference to the cricket authorities, and also as a means of controlling the summer activities of rugby players, that a close-season was first introduced by the Rugby Union following the 1889 AGM. Proposed by A. B. Perkins (Bradford) and seconded by Reverend Marshall, rugby activities were thereby curtailed from 1 May until 31 August (inclusive), and any player transgressing *"close-time"*, as it was known, was deemed to be a professional. A year later a complete check was made on the many 6 and 9-a-side summer rugby competitions, for which prizes were given, by banning games of less than 15-a-side, where a gate was taken, during the close-season. Consequently, there were a small number of suspensions due to these restrictions.

If close-time could be seen to be mutually beneficial to both the rugby and cricketing fraternities, one aspect of the Rugby Union's 1886 professional regulations was deemed to be an infringement, both on the rugby player's amateur freedoms, and of the right of a professional cricketer to play with the club of his choosing. Bearing in mind that there were many joint rugby and cricket clubs, particularly in Yorkshire, the assumption, made by the framers of these first professional regulations, was that clubs would be able to pay a player a substantial amount for his cricketing services, whether as a player or a groundsman, on the understanding that he would also play rugby for the same club during the winter. One rugby official believed that this could be as much as three times his true value. But as one commentator remarked:

*The rugby rulers appear to think that a cricket club would be idiotic enough to play and pay a dummy cricketer as a recognition of football worth. Cricket committees are not built that way, as the football folk could soon find out if they saw fit to inquire.*

Paddock Cricket and Football Club applied to the Yorkshire Rugby Union committee on 5 November, 1889 for a decision on the position of Lorryman, whom they employed as a paid groundsman. As this was the first case to be brought (under Section A Rule 2 of the 1886 regulations) the committee took a lenient view, believing that Paddock had acted in ignorance. They decided that Lorryman, who, in consequence, later joined Brighouse Rangers, could not play for the rugby section but that the club should not be suspended.

E. Southall, the honorary secretary of the cricket section of the Leeds C.F. & A. C. at Headingley, and a rugby player for the same club, was not so fortunate. In effect, Southall professionalised himself when he had the following letter, dated 13 October, 1890, published by the *Yorkshire Post*:

*What constitutes a professional footballer?*

*I fear I am a great reprobate! In the first place I was elected hon. secretary to the Leeds Cricket Club and I actually accepted the post without first consulting the Yorkshire Rugby Union Football Committee. However, I endeavoured to do my duty to the best of my ability, and I succeeded so well that at the close of the cricket season the Cricket Committee voted me the sum of £5 as a recompense for the money that I was out of pocket. In an evil hour I accepted the money, never for a moment anticipating the dreadful consequences that have arisen through so doing. Soon after I was solicited to play football for the Leeds Club, of which I am a full member, and at last consented, and I have actually had the audacity to play, but in so doing have brought down the vengeance of the "Star Chamber" upon myself! I have been excommunicated from the Leeds Football Club! I have been condemned and sentenced without being heard, and the sentence is that I must pay back the £5 I received from the Cricket Committee or become a professional footballer! Let my case, however, be a warning to other cricketers. They will see now that the rugby committee are assuming authority over cricket. In some cricket clubs money prizes are given for catches, wickets bowled, and other feats. Let cricketers beware. The eyes of the authorities are upon them! But, let me ask seriously could any one imagine a number of mature men discussing together such a trivial matter in the nineteenth century and coming to such a ridiculous conclusion?*

After refusing to attend the Yorkshire committee meeting on 22 October, 1889, which consequently declared him a professional, Southall wrote another letter to the *Yorkshire Post*, as follows:

*Referring to Mr Marshall's statement last night, though I have a straightforward and honourable case, which will bear the strictest investigation, I prefer to sacrifice football altogether rather than submit to the indignity of appearing before the County Committee. If Law 2 can be applied to my case, the sooner the revision of that rule takes place the better it will be for the interests of Rugby football.*

It was not to be, however, and Yorkshire three-quarter, Arthur "Sandy" Bairstow - who, as well as stumping for Yorkshire also signed for Bolton Wanderers in 1901 as a goalkeeper - also fell foul of this *"absurd, illogical, unfair and tyrannical restriction"* during his rugby and cricket careers with Bradford and Keighley, despite both clubs having entirely separate club sections.

Perhaps this absurdity is also heightened by the fact that Reverend Marshall - who, of course, agreed whole-heartedly with these restrictions - would be proud to announce in the school magazines from 1885, that professional cricketers, John and Tom Thewlis, from the famous family of hand-loom weavers from Lascelles Hall, had been engaged on a daily basis for the coaching of his pupils.[6]


Those favouring a kicking game were given a head start over rugby by the formation of the F.A. in 1863, and the inauguration of the F.A. Cup for the 1871/2 season. Much of this initial advantage, however, was lost due to the fact that it was not until March, 1877 that universal rules - based on the games at Harrow, Uppingham, and the Sheffield Association - were adopted throughout the whole of England. In 1873, for example, when there were 28 entries, the Engineers' versus Sheffield tie was played one half under London rules and one half under Sheffield rules. Southern clubs, composed of ex-public school boys, dominated the early years of this competition, helped by the fact that, north of Sheffield, there was no great interest taken in non-handling games during the F.A.'s first decade of existence.

The catalyst in Lancashire appears to have been the work of ex-Harrovians, with the first club in that county, at Turton in 1871, *"Monkey"* Hornby's side in Blackburn and Darwen (which at one time also played rugby) all being formed under Harrow rules. At the formation of the Lancashire Football Association on 28 September, 1878, all the 28 founder members - excluding those from neighbouring Church, Turton, Haslingden, and Rawtenstall - came from the towns of Bolton, Darwen and Blackburn. It was no coincidence that this body was formed only months after Darwen lost to the Old Etonians in the fourth round of the 1878/9 F.A. Cup.[7] Darwen's achievement not only provided the stimulus for further expansion of the game in Lancashire, but it also gave a clear indication that the supremacy of the gentleman amateurs was nearing its end. In 1882 Blackburn Rovers became the first non-London club to reach the final, and after Blackburn Olympic beat the Old Etonians in 1883 the Cup was never to be won again by an amateur side.

These national successes, and the introduction of the Lancashire F.A.'s own cup competition in 1879, resulted in a belt of central-Lancashire towns rejecting rugby in favour of soccer. Preston North End (who were originally a rugby club formed by members of the cricket club of the same name) decided to switch entirely to soccer prior to playing their F.A. Cup-tie against Blackburn Rovers in 1881; Burnley (formerly Rovers formed in 1876) embraced soccer in 1882; and Chorley and Bury (both formed in 1875 as rugby clubs) made the move to soccer in 1883 and 1885, respectively.

The achievements of Blackburn Olympic, Blackburn Rovers, and Darwen, were partly attributed to the importation of Scotsmen - adept at a close-passing game rather than the individual dribbles then in vogue - who were ostensibly lured south by the prospect of higher wages in these central Lancashire mill towns. However, with most Lancashire clubs advertising for players in Glasgow newspapers, and with increasing numbers of these Scottish *"professors"* in English club sides, suspicions were raised about their amateur status.

Darwen was one of the first clubs to introduce Scotsmen with J. Love and later F. Suter transferring from Partick in 1878; whilst Archie and Andy Hunter went to Birmingham; and Peter Andrews and James Lang moved to Heeley, and Sheffield Wednesday, respectively, around 1876. The latter Glaswegian is generally regarded to be the first ever soccer professional, having been found a sinecure in Sheffield.[8]

The local Associations carried out their own inquiries and dealt with offending clubs until the scandals became such that the F.A. were forced to act. In 1881 the Lancashire F.A. forbade the signing on of Scots, regardless of whether they were drawn south for employment or football This resulted in Great Lever and Burnley being suspended for having six and seven Scots respectively in their sides. The Birmingham F.A. also expelled players from Walsall and Birmingham St. George.

The F.A. then set up the first of its many sub-committees to look into professionalism, but initially failed to unearth sufficient evidence, although it was apparently well-known that clubs in Lancashire kept a duplicate set of books in order to conceal illegal payments and falsify gate returns. In 1882 the F.A. gave itself power to expel any club which paid its players more than actual expenses or wages lost, i.e. broken-time; and a year later Accrington were expelled from the F.A. after being found guilty of inducing a player named Beresford.

The inevitable escalation came with the inquiry into Preston North End, following *"The Invincibles"* Cup-tie on 9 January, 1884 with southern amateurs, Upton Park, the latter having alleged that Preston had professionals in their side. Far from denying this, at the F.A. inquiry which followed, Major William Suddell, a cotton manufacturer, who had founded the Preston club, openly admitted that his players were paid. Furthermore, he said that he could prove that this was common practice among all the leading clubs in Lancashire and the Midlands. Preston were subsequently thrown out of the competition, and the battle lines were now firmly drawn between the amateur and professional factions within the F.A.

Professionalism had been rejected at a general meeting of the F.A. in February, 1884, following which rules were formulated *"for the repression"* of *"veiled professionalism"* and the importation of players and in June 1884 clubs could not pay their players more than one day's broken-time in any one week, with official receipts being required. The F.A. committee, against all the laws of natural justice, was also empowered to place the onus on clubs to prove their innocence. In October, 1884 they sent out a circular compelling clubs to submit names of all their imported players, together with the wages such players were receiving and the amounts they received at their previous residence.[9]

This was the final straw which led clubs in Lancashire, under the chairmanship of William Suddell, to set in motion the formation of a breakaway British National Association to *"embrace clubs and players of every nationality"*. At the initial meeting on 10 October, 1884 in Bolton seven of the nine Lancashire clubs decided to withdraw from the F.A. Cup and other clubs were advised not to complete the circular. At the third meeting in Manchester, on 30 October, 1884, seventy clubs were represented, including Aston Villa and Sunderland, and with spread of professionalism to the Midlands strengthening the Lancashire cause, the F.A. were compelled to appoint yet another sub-committee to look into the issue.

Its report recommended the introduction of professionalism and that professionals should be allowed to play in the F.A. Cup. However, at general meetings in January and March, 1885, these proposals did not receive the necessary two-thirds majority. Before the latter meeting dispersed, however, a sub-committee was formed with a view to reaching a compromise, and their report, which echoed the motion of the F.A. secretary, Charles. W. Alcock, the previous November: *"That it is expedient to legalise professionalism under stringent conditions, but that no paid player shall take part in the Association Cup competition"*, was finally approved at a sparsely attended general meeting in July, 1885.

It is perhaps worth recording the statement made by Alcock at the meeting in March, and to compare it with the attitudes expressed below from two prominent members of the Rugby Union heirachy who opposed broken-time:

*I cannot be called a supporter of professionalism....but until professionalism is legalized the deadlock which now exists will continue. I consider that veiled professionalism is the evil to be repressed, and I am sure that it now exists in nearly every football district, "pure" Birmingham not excepted. Professionals are a necessity to the growth of the game and I object to the idea that they are utter outcasts some people represent them to be. Furthermore, I object to the idea that it is immoral to work for a living, and I cannot see why men should not, with that object, labour at football as at cricket.*[10]

In view of Alcock's cricketing background - the Old Harrovian was also secretary of Surrey Cricket Club - it is not surprising to find that some of the restrictions placed on the soccer professional included a two-year residential qualification for the F.A. Cup and other inter-county competitions, and the requirement that he should be registered annually with the F.A. and only allowed to play for one club. It was because of this conciliatory approach to the problem of professionalism by Alcock and other leading figures in the soccer establishment, however, that the F.A. was able to avoid the sort of split which was later to occur in rugby.

Nonetheless, following the formation of the fully-professional Football League in 1888, whose financial problems we shall come to later, the F.A. was to face many conflicts of interest between its professional and amateur exponents, culminating in a rift in 1907. This was caused by the F.A. insisting that the London F.A. should open its doors to professional clubs, as was the ruling and practice in other parts of the country. This, however, was too much to bear for the amateur diehards in the Old Boys clubs in Middlesex and Surrey, who decided instead to play among their own class and form the Amateur Football Association.

They were no doubt encouraged by the all-conquering and stylish Corinthians, who had been formed in 1883 by N.L. *"Pa"* Jackson.[11] His reason for establishing this exclusive club - open only to public school and University players - was in order to compete more successfully at international level. Such was their success that they regularly supplied a majority of players for the England side and in exhibition games ran up large scores against the top professional sides of the day. In 1884, for instance, they were able to defeat Blackburn Rovers by 8-1 whilst they also beat the Barbarians at rugby in 1892. Their marked superiority was put down to the fact that, unlike the majority of the professionals, they had played organised games from boyhood, and had further advantages in the way of the best housing, food, and medical advice. Furthermore, they were not inhibited by the need to win league points or cups, which allowed them to play with adventure and flair.

The Corinthians and many other scratch amateur sides, however, were riddled with hypocrisy. As well as benefiting from the large match guarantees, which only the gate-taking professional clubs could provide, their reputation also enabled them to undertake lucrative tours on the Continent. It was apparently the Corinthians whom "*Monkey*" Hornby was alluding to, when, at the Lancashire Rugby Union meeting in 1893, he alleged that, "*they asked larger guarantees than professional clubs, published no balance sheets, and distributed expenses surpassing the wages commanded by professionals.*" [12]

"*Pa*" Jackson might not have agreed with Hornby over these financial matters, but he did admit that he expected professional footballers to adhere to the cricket practice of touching their forelock and addressing the skipper as "*Sir*". He had complained to the F.A. in 1890/1 over their selection of a professional captain for England when there were amateurs in the side; and he later confirmed that the amateurs resisted dining with professionals until circumstances dictated otherwise in 1898. [13]

By depriving themselves of fixtures against the professionals after 1907 the Corinthians soon went into decline and lost their places in the international sides. Another major effect of their demise was the fact that most of the newer schools, without an amateur model to refer to, opted for the socially-fashionable rugby game.

By 1893, the rugby fraternity were, of course, well aware of the history of the struggle in the sister game, and particularly the effect which the Football League and full-time professionalism, including summer wages, was having on the financial affairs of the Football League clubs. Soccer's financial management, and the effects of professionalism - which, ironically, would be used by both sides of rugby's broken-time argument to prove their point - will be referred to in detail later. For the moment, however, it might be as well to examine the reasons why the middle-class attitude towards professionalism in soccer, and the prospect of its adoption in rugby - broken-time being considered by its opponents as *"the thin edge of the wedge of professionalism"* - differed markedly to its acceptance in cricket. This not only applied to the southern middle-class rugby establishment but northern middle-class sports editors.

Rowland Hill, for example, had this to say:

*I am often met in discussing this question with the statement that professionalism has not worked badly in cricket; to this I give my assent, but I decline to admit that cricket and football can be dealt with on parallel lines. As stated above, a man can only play football in good form for a few years, and then he has nothing to fall back upon; whilst a cricketer can retain his form for a long number of years, and when getting on in years he can still be a ground bowler, a teacher of the game, a ground man or an umpire, so that through cricket a man can get genuine occupation for a number of years.*[14]

And Arthur Budd, whilst conveniently ignoring the *"shamateurism"* of Grace and Stoddart, added:

*Our best amateur cricketers devote quite as much time to it as the professionals. As a consequence, while they are able to maintain an equality of play, they are at the same time able to retain a monopoly of government. But if W. G. Grace, A. N. Hornby, A. E. Stoddart, and others could not, by their constant devotion to the game, keep pace with the professionals as competitors, the power of governing would leave them with their inferiority of play.*[15]

One Yorkshire news editor in 1886, however, placed a rather different emphasis on the time needed to master the game of rugby, and thereby exposed the underlying reasons for this middle-class abhorrence of the prospect of professionalism in the game:

*There is really no place for the professional at football. He cannot be a teacher of the game like his cricket brother; indeed, to draw a parallel between the two is absurd. In the one instance the game is indulged in on the Saturday half-holiday only, while the other is followed every day in the week. Nine cricket clubs out of ten of any pretensions whatever engage professionals for instruction and to look after the grounds, but such a thing is absolutely unnecessary in the winter pastime, the rudiments of which can be acquired by any one in half-an-hour, while practice alone will bring proficiency. Then again, a football match only occupies some 90 minutes to decide and not days as in the case of cricket, while the turf requires no attention. The professional in football would encourage idleness, and would engender betting, while men would naturally sell their services to the highest bidder.*[16]

On the one hand, therefore, Rowland Hill and Arthur Budd argued that the amateur could not compete with the professional because of the time allowed for practice. On the other hand, however, the sports editor in 1886 is asking us to believe that rugby required no more than half-an-hour's practice a week, which, if this was so, the amateur gentlemen would surely have had little to fear in terms of competing on purely play performance. Whichever argument we accept both appear to be symtomatic of the same middle-class fear, epitomised by the Northern Union's work clauses in 1898, namely, that the working-class player would become a *"loafer"* or *"idle waster"*, either during his career or in retirement, with time on his hands to get up to all kinds of social unrest during a period of escalating class conflict.[17]

It has been pointed out that Rowland Hill was, in effect, admitting that the rugby establishment were socially inferior to their cricket counterparts, in that, because they had no inherited wealth, they could not afford the time to practice. Most of rugby's southern rulers, sociologists Dunning and Sheard argue, had attended the newer public schools and were therefore less socially secure than their cricket and soccer counterparts.[18] True to their theory, as we have seen, the loudest voice in Lancashire, both in exposing the hypocrisy of *"shamateurism"* and championing the cause of broken-time for the working man, was Old Harrovian Albert Neilson *"Monkey"* Hornby, and following the Lancashire Rugby Union meeting in 1893, which had just discussed Yorkshire's proposal for broken-time, the situation was perhaps summed up by the following statement:

*When you have men like Hornby and J. H. Payne taking opposite sides on a question like this, depend upon it that a crisis is at hand, and the old order of things may be expected to speedily pass away.*[19]

These words were indeed profound, as, unfortunately, rugby union, at both local and national level, had few officials with Hornby's social background. Unlike the aristocrats on the M.C.C. and the F.A., who were able to accommodate professionalism under their amateur control, all the signs were that rugby's insecure middle-class were not prepared to meet the demands for broken-time for its working-class section - and hence, *"the evil"* of *"veiled professionalism"*, which Alcock saw as a greater problem than open professionalism, would continue to flourish in rugby circles.

# Chapter Four
# Veiled Professionalism

There is documented evidence in the north that during the early 1880s rugby players were compensated by their clubs for broken-time. The game's heroes at that time were also publicly presented with substantial cash testimonials for their past and present services to club, county or country. Neither type of payment appears to have contravened any rules of the Rugby Union, as there was no national definition of what constituted *"professionalism"* until the 1886 regulations (see below), which were an attempt to outlaw all profit from the game, except for testimonials which came under greater scrutiny after 1889.

Leaving aside for the moment the position of the "gentleman" player, about whom we shall conclude this chapter, there were numerous ways in which working-class players were able to benefit from their association with the game during the 1880s and 1890s. Any doubts in the public's mind on this score should have been well and truly erased by the time that *"A Wag"* commented at the end of the 1889/90 season:

*Popularising the game has brought a whole train of difficulties in its wake (viewed at least from the amateur stand-point), difficulties which are neither the outcome of cup-ties nor of any specific style of game, but simply the natural result of the working man's association with the sport. He can never be strictly amateur… and the county committee can no more stop the flow of money into the football artisan's pocket than Canute could stop the waves…How it's done nobody cares, nor whether Jack Brown, the famous three-quarter, spends ten shillings more a week than he can satisfactorily account for to the Rugby Union. It is only when the thing becomes a public scandal that our sensitive natures receive a shock which nothing but a court-martial in committee can remove, and then we see the righteous indignation of our sport-loving rulers set forth in all its vehemence.*

*Meanwhile Tom Smith, the crack forward, who is an engine-tenter by trade, and must have remained so all his life but for football, blossoms forth, by some mysterious process of transformation known only to footballers, into mine host of the Brown Cow, where a roaring trade is done forthwith, varying in extent according to the prowess and popularity of the landlord in the field, whilst a dropped goal or even a try may double the receipts on a Saturday night. Now it is not for me to complain at the existence of these things, which do not in my opinion hurt the game one bit, only do let us be fair and not abuse these struggling men's hospitality by calling them "amateurs"....as soon as we can call a spade a spade in Yorkshire, well, there will be a slight alteration, that's all!* [1]

Reverend Marshall would not agree with *"Wag's"* sentiments, of course, but he confirmed many of the above practices in this extract from an article which he wrote on broken-time in 1891. According to Marshall it would also seem that the sympathetic employer subsidised the game:

*There can be no doubt that in many ways the football player gets some remuneration. His employer allows him to leave work, and does not deduct his wage. This is done in many cases and is perfectly legitimate. There is nothing more in this than an employer allowing leave to a clerk, or a head master giving leave of absence to an assistant master. Again there are little presents and tips from admirers. What is easier than to put half a sovereign or so into a man's hand after playing well in a match? This is done, and cannot be prevented or legislated against. Or for a manufacturer to send in cloth sufficient for a suit or trouser-length as a present. What is wrong in this? Cannot I, if a manufacturer, do this to any friend of mine? There are indeed many and secret ways of remunerating the football player, many that have come to my notice (which would surprise the uninitiated, but that are no secret to many), that it would be impossible to detect, very difficult to condemn, and altogether out of the pale of practical legislation.* [2]

Those methods which it was thought possible to control are to be found in the 1886 regulations and they give, of course, a good indication of the official concerns. Including the practices which will come to light in the inquiries into professionalism, perhaps it is possible to categorize all such benefits to players, as follows: 1) broken-time allowed by employers or broken-time payments paid by clubs, 2) unpaid *"loans"*, 3) testimonials, 4) tours, 5) employment on condition of transferring club, 6) employment related to the drinks trade, 7) inflated expenses, 8) individual match payments and other "boot money", 9) sundry gifts from well-wishers, 10) misuse of insurance schemes.

On the latter point, officials did worry that players would gain financially from such schemes but, of course, they could not deny that there was a need for insurance in such a dangerous game as rugby. According to H. H. Almond, the great increase in the number of accidents to players was attributable to the abolition, in 1872, of the rule that stated, *"The ball might not be taken in the hands except in the case of a free catch or when fairly bounding."* [3] This meant that many more players were subsequently injured due to the necessity to drop on the ball. Although there are no statistics available from the 1870s to show whether this was the case, it is obvious from the evidence during the 1880s and 1890s that players ran a high level of risk of death and serious injury. In 1889 the *Pall Mall Gazette* highlighted the problem by listing nine deaths in as many weeks from January to March, and a return of the number of accidents and fatalities during the three seasons, 1890/1 to 1892/3, showed that there had been a total of 71 deaths, 121 broken legs, 33 broken arms, 54 broken collar bones, and 158 other injuries - the total number of *"deaths and damages"* in the British Isles amounting to 437. This weekly death rate throughout the season had therefore been maintained, and there was apparently no let up in the number of working hours lost through rugby injuries.[4]

Clubs of any standing had seen the need to safeguard against such hazards from the early 1880s, Bradford and Hull, for example, insuring their players in 1883 and 1885, respectively. Bradford's former captain, W. H. Smith, was the agent for an employers' liability scheme which paid the players 15 shillings a week for *"total disablement"* and 7/6d for *"partial disablement"* with the players contributing 25% towards the cost of the premium, whilst in 1885/6 Hull's injured players received an unemployment benefit of £1/10s a week.[5]  It has been impossible to discover how these individual schemes operated in practice or what safeguards were demanded but in 1886 there was some concern that they would fall under the umbrella of the proposed professional regulations.

At the Lancashire meeting which discussed the above proposals, Mr Taylor (Oldham) said that Clause B (see below): *"....would work unfairly with the working-class clubs in Lancashire and Yorkshire...it would be a very great hardship indeed to be designated a professional simply because a man was remunerated for actual services in the work of his club, or if he was injured in the course of a match, that he should not be allowed to receive any compensation without being made a professional."* He therefore proposed, seconded by Mr Conshaw (Wigan), that a club be allowed to compensate for loss of time incurred by reason of injuries in matches, and this was passed unanimously.[6]  The Rugby Union later sanctioned such insurance schemes commencing from the 1886/7 season but Rowland Hill later commented:

*There is nothing in principle wrong in permitting clubs to insure their players; but care must be taken that under the guise of insurance players do not make a profit out of the accident fund.*[7]

Certainly, as regards the north, his concern would prove to be valid, although evidence of specific cases of abuse of the insurance schemes are difficult to unearth. Under new stringent regulations, introduced in February, 1890, powers were delegated to the county commmittees and clubs were allowed to pay a doctor's expenses out of their insurance fund. Thus, with the requirement of a medical certificate, there was presumably less chance of players malingering.[8] It was said, however, that Yorkshire's insurance fund had been *"unjustly imposed upon"* after it made a loss of £370 during 1892 and there were calls for it to be suspended. Perhaps the following case, and others like it, had something to do with this condemnation. It was reported in February, 1893, that a Leeds player was receiving more whilst injured than he could have earned from his regular employment:

> *When working, he gets a pound a week, but the insurance scheme brought him in 38 shillings, for his masters allowed him a third of his wages during sickness...He didn't want to get better, of course!*

This state of affairs was later confirmed at Manningham's 1893 AGM, when, referring to the insurance fund, the secretary said that the club's deficit was attributable almost solely to players, *"who would rather draw 36 shillings...rather than a much less sum and work at their regular employment."* [9]

It had been unsuccessfully proposed in 1891 that injured players should only be paid the amount of their lost wages rather than the full insurance fees, but, in order to further combat the above losses, at the Yorkshire AGM in 1892, a figure of six shillings for each week-day had been set as the maximum compensation. This produced such a satisfactory reduction in the deficit during 1894 that the Yorkshire committee found it in their hearts to make a number of special grants to several injured players. Nonetheless, it was perhaps unwise of James Miller, at the crucial Rugby Union meeting in 1893, to cite the working of the insurance scheme as a means by which broken-time payments could be controlled and administered.

Although not easily fitting into the above categories of remuneration, gambling was clearly part of the environment of northern rugby and there were instances where players apparently gambled on the outcome of games in which they were involved. This subsequently led to some accusations that they were *"throwing"* games for their own financial gain. Bookmakers, who were part of the scene at every amateur athletic meeting until the Street Betting Act of 1907 effectively curbed the practice, also appear to have found plenty of punters on northern rugby grounds from about the time that the Yorkshire Cup competition started to take its effect. On 20 January, 1883, for example, they apparently lost over £50 on the result of the Wakefield-Halifax match, whilst on 24 February, 1883 bookmakers were actually in the Crown Flatt ground, and it was said that, *"Several prominent patrons of the Dewsbury club expressed their disgust at the spectacle and threatened to withdraw their support from the club."* In 1886 it was also reported that Bradford and Halifax supporters were *"laying odds of £90-30 and £80-20"* during the half-time interval at Park Avenue. Dewsbury actually expelled some club members for gambling on games at Crown Flatt in November, 1889, but despite the claim that from about this time the game had become *"purer"* and that there was not, *"a single club in the county that has not taken steps by vigourous action to expel the betting man"*, the problem apparently persisted.[10] At the Yorkshire committee inquiry during September, 1889, *"Dickie"* Lockwood said that one of the reasons why he left Dewsbury was the fact that he had been accused of *"selling"* games, especially the cup-tie with Wakefield Trinity; and Joe Northend, the Leeds Parish Church full-back, went so far as to send a letter, dated 28 September, 1890, to the local newspapers in order to attempt to clear his name due to the rumours surrounding his performance against Bramley in that year's Yorkshire Cup-tie:

*I have been charged so frequently by so many men, who call themselves Parish Church supporters, of receiving so much bribe money not to try in the Bramley cup-tie last year - and they all say that they can prove it...I am open to deposit £10, and will forfeit the same, if they can prove that I have received a half-penny in all my life to throw a match over of any description, particularly a match played after a six weeks' suspension, where all the team was disorganised. The whole team was beaten, but all the blame rests on the full-back!*

Later, at Batley's 1892 AGM a heated discussion took place over the Yorkshire Cup replay with Bramley, when it was alleged by some members that, *"The game (was) "sold" by certain prominent members who had each received £5 in order to bring about the side's defeat"*.[11] None of the above accusations appear to have been substantiated, but, nonetheless, they point to the fact that gambling and monetary values generally paid a large part in the climate of northern rugby.


It has been said that, *"The essential definition of amateurism is freedom"*, and certainly in the 1860s to early 1880s players were largely free to decide on the level of their involvement. *"Monkey"* Hornby's independent nature, which was expressed by his giving priority to a shooting week-end, rather than turning out for the North in 1883, perhaps epitomised this *laissez faire* attitude. Players initially were not strictly attached to any one club but made themselves available to several teams during the season, and this was extremely common prior to the introduction of leagues. They might also make a guest appearance with a neighbouring club on one of their tours. This freedom would include, of course, being able to arrange fixtures against players of one's own class, as with such as Manchester and Liverpool, although the more socially mixed clubs, such as Bradford, were also reluctant to grant fixtures to the newer organisations. It also extended to playing under assumed names - *noms de guerre*, for reasons perhaps known only to themselves, being particularly popular among many *"gentlemen"* players.

Prior to clubs being in a position to charge admission the game was obviously wholly amateur, and even when gate-money was taken, from about the mid-1870s, players doubtless paid a club subscription, provided their own kit, and also paid their own train fares. With fixtures being difficult to arrange and the season not usually starting until well into October and sometimes later, it is unlikely that a middle-class player in the early 1870s would have expended a great deal of his income on the sport. As far as the working-class employee, as distinct from the self-employed tradesman, was concerned, until the introduction of the Saturday half-holiday in 1874 it was more than likely, of course, that the game was beyond his reach. To state this with any confidence, however, much more employment data would be needed on these very early teams.

Shortly after this legislation, the gate-taking clubs started to widen their fixture lists, and there were increasing numbers of inter-county matches from around 1877/8, a season in which Oldham, for example, travelled over the Pennines for the first time. It was from about this time that the artisan's pocket would presumably have been placed under increasing strain, and it is known that sometimes they might have had to rely on the charity of their higher status colleagues. Mark Newsome, for example, apparently paid the fare of a fellow Dewsbury player who could not afford to travel with the team to Swinton.[12]    Theoretically, the burden for those players with any talent would appear to have been much greater, as county trial matches and full county matches were usually played mid-week, and some county and international games entailed two and three days away from home. Furthermore, working men almost certainly would have had to break time on Saturday mornings to play clubs in the next county, all games in those days being played in the afternoons. Without the use of floodlights, and Sunday sport strictly taboo, any re-arrangements due to bad weather, or replayed cup-ties, might also have been replayed during mid-week afternoons.

There were experiments with early floodlighting systems in the 1870s. On 2 November, 1878, for example, Halifax played Birch at Hanson Lane under Siemens Lights, which attracted a crowd estimated at over 20,000, who brought the proceedings to a halt when they invaded the pitch. Gramme's Lights were used for a game between Broughton Rangers and Swinton on 22 October, 1878, whilst St. Helens and Wigan attracted a crowd of 7,000 to Dentons Green Lane on 24 January, 1889 when the pitch was illuminated by twelve Wells Lights. All these systems proved ineffective and unsafe, however, and quickly fell into disuse. Floodlighting was not to be the answer, therefore, and although in the early months of the season matches could obviously kick-off in the early evenings, for the greater part of the season most working men had problems when they were confined to the work place until one o'clock on Saturday afternoons.

Because of work commitments, allied to an inefficient rail network and lackadaisical club managements, the 1880s and 1890s are littered with numerous late starts, broken engagements, and games reduced in length due to the descending darkness. There were also some instances where teams either boarded the wrong train, or left behind their luggage. Huddersfield, for example, turned up at Castleford in 1890 at 5.15 with every man donning a different coloured jersey, which they had hurriedly bought from the local sports outfitters, and most wearing their ordinary shoes! Such unpunctuality was not confined to the players, as it is known that, because of the poor train service, both Barron Kilner (at the Halifax-Leeds game in 1890) and Reverend Marshall (at the first-ever Bradford-Blackheath game in 1886) arrived late to referee games, but there was an expectation that certain teams were always likely to be late-comers. This is epitomised by the fact that several reporters at Parkside in 1891 completely missed the first half of Hunslet's game against Kendal Hornets, due to the Westmorelanders arriving in time for the advertised kick-off! Generally, however, for the crowds and the press, who sometimes had to wait for over an hour in the most appalling weather and on exposed wooden stands and uncovered press boxes, the situation was an intolerable one.

In Rugby Union days the threat of a fixed penalty for unpunctual starters was never carried out, but with the legalisation of broken-time, the Northern Union were not only able to insist on fixed kick-off times depending on the time of year but also the introduction of fines for late starts. Although this was later seen to be one of the greatest improvements to the game in the north, it appears not to have been raised by the supporters of broken-time. Perhaps this was due to the fact that the views of the paying public, of this ostensibly amateur game, were never really considered when changes were being discussed.

Naturally, however, spectators were far more interested in the number of late starts and non-appearance of teams than they were over the issue of broken-time, and in 1891 a Yorkshire newspaper ventured the opinion, *"If they would legislate on late starts rather than raking over the old ashes of professionalism time and again they would please the public more."* The two issues, however, would seem to have been inextricably linked and there is evidence that a decade earlier some clubs were aware of the need to pay their players broken-time in order to facilitate early departures to games.

Wakefield Trinity's minutes for 1881/2, the season in which they appeared in their fourth successive Yorkshire Cup final, record, for example, that on 28 November, 1881 the committee passed the following resolution: *"That broken-time be paid to any player in the first team when the train leaves Wakefield at 1.00 o'clock or after"*. On 19 December, 1881, however, this decision was rescinded when a resolution was carried: *"That for the remainder of the season no money be paid out of funds of the club to any member on account of broken-time and that a notice be posted in the rooms to that effect."* Unfortunately, there is no record of the amount of such payments or why they ceased to be paid so quickly.[13] It would also appear that around this same period such payments were also being made in the south-west, if we are to believe a local speaker, at a dinner held after the England versus Wales exhibition match at Plymouth during February, 1913, who said that, *"Broken-time payments have been made in these parts for 30 years, and I find the Northern Union the purer amateur body."* [14]

Such a value judgement, of course, is impossible to prove and the discovering of other evidence, that payments to players took place, also presents considerable problems. It is unlikely that after 1886 clubs would have been foolish enough to have recorded broken-time payments in their books, although in November, 1890, Warrington apparently granted bonuses of two shillings and sixpence and one shilling to their first and second teams, respectively, for the games against Rochdale Hornets, and put this on record in their minutes.[15]

For the most part, therefore, we have to rely on the testimony of journalists who professed to having such close relationships with the players, that the latter were quite willing to divulge the levels of such illegal payments. For example, writing in November, 1890, *"Athlete"* had this to say:

*There is no need for professionalism to the same extent as in association football, yet arrangements could be made whereby a player who simply leaves his town to better themselves - even if work is found through his abilities as a footballer - may be allowed to pose as an amateur.....I have had the opportunity of securing the opinions of some of the best players in England on the question and not a single one of them has disagreed with me when I have remarked "That professionalism would always be present in some form or other." The authorities are perfectly aware that the game cannot be confined to amateurs. I myself know a certain player who received £5 for a single match and I could mention several other cases...*[16]

The press itself, however, might also have needed to place its trust in the inside informant or rumour monger, as, for example, in 1886 when Batley's players were said to have benefited from the game at Barrow. *"There is a grave rumour afloat about the Batley team, and it is not without some foundation. Is it true that the half of the gate for the match at Barrow which was handed over to Batley was shared amongst the fifteen who played?"*

Such intrigues, of course, were at the very heart of *"veiled professionalism"*, although, in the late 1870s to the mid-1880s there were certainly other cash payments to players which were both overt and perfectly legal.

It was one of the traditions of the northern game for the public to honour their heroes with testimonials, either for cup-winning feats or international appearances, for long service rendered to their club, as a wedding gift, or to help players who had lost work through injuries. These usually took the form of a purse of gold sovereigns and other smaller tokens of appreciation. There was nothing in the north to match the £600 which Welsh international Arthur Gould received in 1897[17], but a few examples from the late 1870s to mid-1880s should suffice to show that there were several leading players who received enough money either to furnish their house or to help establish them in a small business.

After having his hand amputated following a rugby injury in 1876, Halifax's 21-year old forward Mr Major Brown had to retire both from the game and his job as an apprentice wool buyer. Being one of Halifax's founders he was extremely popular and his testimonial reached £50 (approximately £2,500 at 1984 prices), which helped him open a tobacconist's shop near the ground in Hanson Lane. He was Halifax's first representative on the Yorkshire Senior Competition in 1892/3, and later took to refereeing. Jimmy Dodd, Halifax's captain and centre three-quarter, was awarded a testimonial in July 1883 in the form of 100 sovereigns and a marble clock, although he went on to play until 1893 when in his 40th year. Still only 24 years of age, Fred Bonsor, the Bradford half-back and captain, who played for England in all three internationals in 1885/6, was publicly presented with a purse of gold valued at £80 and a keyless half-hunter gold watch after the home game against Liverpool on 2 October, 1886. That same month, Halifax's leading three-quarter, Tom Scarborough, who was emigrating to Australia, received 100 guineas and other valuables after the game against Broughton Rangers.

Testimonial accounts came under greater official scrutiny after 1889 when Wakefield Trinity's C. E. *"Teddy"* Bartram became the first player to be professionalised in connection with a retirement benefit. His case highlighted the fact that clubs could attempt to disguise illegal payments to players in the form of unpaid loans, and this brought a spate of convictions due to clubs contributing directly to these funds. W. F. B. Calvert, Hull's county half-back from 1882-4, for example, was professionalised in September, 1889 and failed to be reinstated in December 1892. In 1890 he kept the Plimsoll Hotel in Witham. During September of that year, W. I. Fawcett of Manningham was deemed to be a professional after receiving a cash benefit in order that he could buy a piano prior to emigrating to America. Having had second thoughts about this move he unsuccessfully sought to be reinstated, and a month later it was reported that he was, *"kicking cows instead of goals in Manitoba"*. By October, 1894, however, he had returned to Bradford and taken tenancy of the Peel Hotel. A. J. Moore of Silsden, near Keighley, accepted the proceeds from a testimonial match and was professionalised in 7 February, 1891. On his first appeal he failed to be reinstated although, around the same period, Samuel Hall was only suspended for receiving £25 on leaving Swinton. Said to have been *"at death's door"* and in great need of assistance, former Halifax player George Scholefield (whose job as a telegraph clerk had apparently allowed him plenty of time for training during the day) was granted a testimonial in February, 1892. As the presentation was made by his friends in the form of £70 in cash, however, the Halifax club, who were anxious to free themselves of any blame over a transaction in which they were not directly involved, recommended to the Yorkshire committee that Scholefield should be declared a professional. Subsequently, this was agreed to and Halifax were quite rightly exonerated of any blame.[18] To professionalise a critically ill man, however, seems a rather harsh measure, and in order to see how this change in attitude towards cash testimonials took place within English rugby we now need to slightly retrace our steps.

As the game reached the mid-1880s it was clear that the previously unwritten *"amateur ethos"* in rugby was no longer relevant to the changing circumstances in the north. Inevitably, it was the demands of the Yorkshire Cup (the rules of which, at that time, only allowed for teams to be composed of *bona fide* amateur players) and the need for clubs to recruit local players and *"import"* others from as far away as Wales, which proved to be the catalyst for the first national legislation against so-called professionalism.

There had been earlier complaints that players were being poached by clubs, but Manningham had the distinction of being the first club to be charged when, after the first round of the Yorkshire Cup in 1886, Pudsey appealed on the grounds that Manningham had played two *"professionals"*, ex-Selby players W. Pulleyn and J. Birmingham. At the Yorkshire committee meeting held on 1 March, a Mr Ullathorne stated that Pulleyn, who was formerly apprenticed to him as a joiner until 12 October, 1885, had frequently broken time in order to play for Manningham. On one occasion, it was alleged, Pulleyn held up a postal order and said: *"Who will work here when he gets paid for football?"* This was confirmed by a former workmate of Pulleyn's, who said that the player, who had been out of work during the rugby season, had boasted that the postal orders had been sent by Manningham. The vice-president of Selby told the committee that he had used his influence to get some stone-breaking work for Birmingham, but the half-back had told him that he was getting 28 shillings a week from Manningham, which was 10 shillings more than he could earn at this back-breaking work.

In a sworn declaration Manningham's officials denied that either player had received a single penny for their services, other than out-of-pocket travelling expenses, and that, *"no subterfuge, or stratagem had been resorted to for evading the regulation (Rule 4 of the Yorkshire Challenge Cup rules) against payment of players"*. A similar affidavit was also signed by both players. Manningham admitted, however, that some members of the club had promised employment to Pulleyn, who told the committee that such work was on condition that he played for the club. Subsequently he had been employed at three joinery firms. It emerged that Birmingham was invited to play for Manningham by the club captain, W. I. Fawcett, who *"accidentally"* met him in Selby during the previous summer. Birmingham said that he came to Manningham because they were a better club and in order to earn better wages, but denied ever saying that he had been offered 28 shillings a week to play with them. After a brief deliberation the county committee found that, *"...the evidence laid before them fails to prove that either of the two players in question has received any money from Manningham, over and above his third-class rail fare.*[19]

At this stage, therefore, it was not illegal to seduce a player with the prospect of better employment, and it was a widely held view, even after the practice was outlawed, that there was little wrong with such an arrangement, a rugby player having a legitimite right to move to areas where he might have better work prospects. For those in authority, however, such migrations were invariably viewed with a suspicious eye and were felt to be at the root of the problem of *"veiled professionalism."*

Following this first case A. E. Hudson, the Yorkshire President, added:

*Every committee member was determined that the same "scandal" which had obtained in the Association game should not creep into the rugby game in*

*Yorkshire. Whenever a case of professionalism was proved they would deal severely with it, and they felt sure that they could rely on the support of all clubs, who had the interests of the game at heart in their determination to prevent the introduction of any such vitiation.*

It was not that surprising that it should be a Yorkshireman, albeit an exiled Yorkshireman, George T. Thomson, who proposed, at the Rugby Union general meeting on 31 March, 1886, that the question of professionalism should be examined. A former Halifax woollen merchant, educated at Heath Grammar School, he was the first Yorkshireman to be elected as a vice-president on the Rugby Union. This was in 1885, a year in which he made his international debut and also moved to London as a commission agent. Subsequently he served on a sub-committee, along with F. I. Currey (the Rugby Union President), J. MacLaren (Manchester and Lancashire), Arthur Budd (Blackheath), William Cail (Northumberland), A. E. Hudson (Leeds), H. W. T. Garnett (Otley and Yorkshire), and G. Rowland Hill, the latter who circulated the proposed rules to clubs prior to them coming up for discussion at the AGM on 4 October, 1886. These read as follows:

1. *Professionalism is illegal.*
2. *A professional is (a) Any player who shall receive from his club, or any member of it, any money consideration whatever, actual or prospective for services rendered to the club of which he is a member. Note - This sub-section is to include any money consideration, paid or given to any playing member, whether as Secretary, Treasurer, or other officer of the club, or for work or labour of any sort done on or about the ground or in connection with the club's affairs. (b) Any player who receives any compensation for loss of time, from his club or any member of it. (c) Any player trained at the club's expense, or at the expense of any member of the club. (d) Any player who transfers his services from one club to another on the consideration of any contract, engagement, or promise on the part of a club, or any member of that club, to find him employment. (e) Any player who receives from his club, or any member of it, any sum in excess of the amount actually disbursed by him on account of hotel or travelling expenses incurred in connection with the club's affairs.*
3. *The R.F.U. Committee shall have the power of suspending for as long as they think fit (a) Any player whom they consider to be a professional and b) Any club which shall in their opinion have been proved to have played a professional after the 15th day of October, 1886.*
4. *The R.F.U. Committee shall have the power of suspending: (a) Any club which shall have a match with a club which has been suspended by them under Rule 3, or with any club which has been formed out of the nucleus of any suspended club, and (b) Any club which has employed any of its paid servants as umpire, or employed any umpire who has received any sum in excess of the amount*

*actually disbursed by him on account of hotel or travelling expenses.*
5. *An inquiry in any suspected instance of a breach by any club of any of these rules may be instituted by the R.F.U. Committee (a) In their absolute discretion. (b) At the request of any club which may lodge a complaint. In the event of an inquiry being instituted at the complaint of a club, such club shall deposit with the hon. secretary of the Rugby Union the sum of £10.*
6. *On any inquiry the R.F.U. Committee shall have the power to require the production of any books, documents, or evidence, on oath or otherwise, which they deem necessary or desirable.*
7. *In the event of any club declining or neglecting to submit to, or appear at, or co-operate in any inquiry, or to furnish such evidence as may be required, the R.F.U. Committee shall have the power to suspend such club.*

Explaining the need for such regulations the *Yorkshire Post* remarked:

*At present in Yorkshire the sport has fallen to a pitiful state through the shameful practices that have been permitted to obtain a hold upon it in certain teams we could mention. The members of these fifteens have looked upon the game as a profitable means of livelihood....A match, and especially a game in action with the Challenge Cup competition, must be the win, tie, or wrangle, principle, a defeat meaning much depreciation as a saleable, marketable commodity to each of the hired players on the losing side. Referees decisions have been called into question and these functionaries assaulted, and frivolous objections made on every possible point and opportunity....That Yorkshire is mainly responsible for the prevailing state of things no one who has paid any attention to the matter will dare to gainsay....With the crowds considerable betting has arisen, while all kinds of sharp practices have quickly followed - a fact which the records of the past season prove. We have had during recent years continual complaints of men seduced from one club to another, of unseemly disputes, and of rough play, the result undoubtedly of the anxiety evinced by the various clubs to get together a strong team for these competitions, regardless of how and from what quarters they are procured.*[20]

Their latter remarks were indeed apt for the first player migrations from Wales were beginning to occur following Dewsbury's tour to the Principality earlier in the year. Consequently, after making their debuts in the defeat of Castleford on 18 September, 1886, Cardiff's international half-back, William James Wood *"Buller"* Stadden, and Angus J. Stuart, a three-quarter of Scottish descent (who, against Gloucester in 1884, had been a member of the first-ever four three-quarter line in first-class rugby), both appeared before the Yorkshire Committee on 1 October, 1886. They were there to answer the allegations that they were being paid better wages in their adopted town on the condition that they played for Dewsbury.

A former labourer, Stadden, who made the first of his eight

appearances for Wales against Ireland in 1884 and had played against England and Scotland earlier in the year, had moved to Dewsbury at the end of May, 1886. He was followed by his Cardiff colleague and both were found employment, Stuart having left his trade as a draper to become a blanket "*raiser*" at the blanket manufacturers, Newsome, Son & Speddings, of which firm Mark Newsome, the Dewsbury representative on the county committee and the seconder of the broken-time proposal in 1893, was a partner.

After the departure of their two former players Cardiff communicated the facts to the Welsh Rugby Union, who in turn passed on their findings to the English Rugby Union. As the latter, at that time, had no power to settle the controversy the matter was left in abeyance to await the outcome of the Rugby Union's AGM. Following this Stadden and Stuart were granted their transfers and both were in the side which beat Leeds St. John's on Tuesday, 12 October, 1886 at Crown Flatt to celebrate the laying of Dewsbury Town Hall's foundation stone.

Stadden, who later became first a butcher and then a licencee, went on to play for Yorkshire on 21 occasions. He chose not to play for Wales at Llanelli in 1887 for fear that he might lose his eligibility for the Yorkshire Cup ties, but he had the distinction of scoring the only try of the match when Wales beat England for the first time in their history at a snow-swept Crown Flatt in 1890.

At the Lancashire AGM on 2 October, 1886 Manchester and Barrow were among the clubs who entirely supported the sub-committee's professional proposals. However, there was strong opposition from other quarters with one delegate actually proposing unsuccessfully that: "*A man receiving broken-time incurred in playing matches should not be branded a professional*". This is perhaps one of the first public statements in England advocating broken-time payments in rugby, and perhaps a clear indication that it was a common practice at this particular (unnamed) Lancashire club.[21]

The above professional rules, which were moved by A. E. Hudson at the Rugby Union AGM and passed by the majority of the 89 clubs present, came into effect from 15 October, 1886. There were less than ten votes against the proposals with the main dissenting voice appearing to come from Horace Lyne, the future President of the Welsh Rugby Union and Newport's delegate to the English Rugby Union - the club enjoyed dual status until 1897 when they resigned over the A. J. Gould affair - who expressed the view that the rules were too stringent. A champion of the working-class player, he appears to have been the only one at the meeting who advocated broken-time payments, although this was, of course, strongly fancied by at least one Lancashire club.

In February, 1890, the Rugby Union committee not only decided to delegate to county committees the various powers under the 1886 regulations but also passed the following resolutions relating to testimonials, suspensions, and professional soccer players:

*(a) Every testimonial to any member connected with a football club belonging to the Union is illegal, and both the giver and receiver shall be considered as infringing the laws of professionalism unless the presentation has been sanctioned by the county committee.. (b) No man who has been suspended or has contravened the regulations ...as regards to professionalism shall either play, umpire or referee without first obtaining the sanction of the Union committee. (c) Any player registered as a professional under the rules of the F.A. is a professional within the meaning of the regulations of the Union with regards to professionalism.*

As we shall see in chapter six these additional restrictions almost immediately followed the suspensions of Wakefield Trinity's C. E. Bartram and Heckmondwike's J. W. Sutcliffe, the latter who had found refuge with Bolton Wanderers.

The fight against *"veiled professionalism"* was further intensified with the introduction at the Rugby Union's 1891 AGM of new transfer rules. These were largely the work of Reverend Marshall, in whose eyes there existed two recognised classes of player, *"those who played for the sake of the game, and those whose conduct was open to suspicion"*. He explained that the principle upon which the rules were drafted was, *"to empower the counties to deal with suspects and be sufficiently elastic as to safeguard the right of the amateur to play with whichever club they chose".*[22] In a reversal of natural justice, however, whenever a club failed to agree to a player's transfer, either locally or in another county or country, the onus was placed on the player to fully satisfy the county committee as to the *bona fide* character of the transfer. Failing a satisfactory explanation there were a number of powers open to the committee, namely, to refuse the transfer, suspend the prospective club or player, or declare the player a professional. The effect of these new rules is also covered in chapter six.

The one area, which the Rugby Union's professional regulations and transfer rules did not reach, was the arrangement by which clubs were able to have players installed as licensees and billiard hall managers. Rugby's connections with the drinks trade goes back to the 1870s when many clubs were formed at meetings held in pubs and hotels. Most clubs from the outset had their headquarters and dressing-rooms in licensed premises, either adjacent or near to the ground. If it was in walking distance the players and officials would have to risk the wrath of the crowd on foot, if the ground was slightly further afield they might be driven there on match days by horse-drawn waggonette. This latter tradition survived until well into the 1900s by which time the dressing-rooms were mostly accommodated on the grounds. The public house, however, still remained as the main focal point for the club and its supporters.

During an address given in Leeds in  the speaker described (rugby) football as, *"a fascination of the devil and twin sister of the drinking system, without the latter of which it would have a job to succeed"*. Needless to say, most rugby followers in the audience chose to walk out! To support their moral crusade the Yorkshire Church Temperance Committee donated a Challenge Shield from 1887. Initially it was open to church clubs, which, although they could have their dressing-rooms at licensed premises, agreed to hold their general or annual meetings elsewhere. With most clubs having their headquarters in public houses, however, and many rugby players being installed as publicans or employed as waiters, the above committee were fighting a losing battle. Consequently, in 1893/4, the temperance clause was struck out and the competition was open to all junior clubs. The winners of the Temperance Shield in 1892/3 were Leeds Parish Church and, ironically, their captain George Mosley and his fellow half-back, *"Paddy"* Ryan, were both publicans![23]

In rugby football therefore the devil and the drinks trade were certainly winning. This was a fact which Reverend Marshall referred to at the broken-time meeting when he pointed out that at one club in Yorkshire there were seven publicans (from available evidence this would appear to be a close run thing between Bradford and Halifax) and during the previous season eleven Yorkshire players had jobs connected with breweries. Marshall was not exaggerating as in the list of 35 players who represented the county in 1892/3 the following are known to have been licensees: R. E. Lockwood (Heckmondwike), Albert Goldthorpe (Hunslet), T. Summersgill (Leeds), D. Jowett (Heckmondwike), W. Nichol (Brighouse), J. Toothill (Bradford), H. Bradshaw (Bramley), H. Speed (Castleford), F. Lowrie (Batley), and Arthur Briggs (Bradford) who was a landlord in Stockport during March, 1893 at the same public house formerly occupied by Saville, the Stockport captain. Furthermore, E. Hudson (Hunslet) was a billiard hall manager, and Mark Fletcher (Leeds) was a waiter at the Lord Nelson Hotel, Kirstall Road, which had been a popular haunt for rugby players for a number of years. In 1889, for example, Robert Walton, St. John's three-quarter, said that he earned 18 shillings a week there as a waiter. Of the other Yorkshire players in 1892/3, E. Redman (Manningham) moved into a public house during the following season on transferring to Leicester, maltster Tom Broadley (Bradford) later became a life-long

71

licensed victualler, and former coal miner Harry Varley (Liversedge) took over the Gardner's Arms, Cross Street, on his transfer to Oldham in September, 1893.

Lancashire's leading clubs, in fact, also appear to have had little difficulty in arranging such situations for players. For example, in 1890 former Rochdale Hornets' county half-back, John Nolan was installed in the Coronation Arms, Mumps, on his transfer to Oldham, and Rochdale were equally successful in obtaining for the former Halifax county half-back, the *"Little Wonder"* Edmund Buckley, the tenancy of the George and Dragon, Blackwater Street, in February, 1894. Oldham's Welsh signing in 1890, David Gwynn, was later landlord of the Prince William of Gloucester, Market Place; Jim Valentine, Swinton's international three-quarter was a licencee for many years; whilst Wigan's half-backs in 1892/3, Mitchinson and county player W. Helliwell, were both Yorkshire, there is little doubt that the installation of players as publicans was a common method adopted to import a leading player on both sides of the Pennines. As we have seen with Saville of Stockport, this also applied to Cheshire, where Runcorn's international full-back in 1892, Sam Houghton, was licensee of the Egerton Arms, Bridge Street.

Whilst Reverend Marshall might have deemed it to be morally reprehensible that the game should be tainted in this way there appears to have been little that the rugby union authorities could do about this phenomenon. Certainly they had to draw the line at banning players who were associated with the drinks trade as they had insufficient funds available to risk a possible court action by the wealthy and powerful brewers.

Clubs which could not quickly arrange a pub vacancy could find that a neighbouring club had secured the player's transfer. Bradford, for example, were said to have lost the prospect of signing two forwards in August, 1893 because they could not arrange pubs for them. They were also expected to sign the Westmorelander, R. S. Winskill, from Kendal Hornets until Halifax arranged for him to take over the Northgate Hotel.[24] Players were not only able to attract custom to their pubs, particularly if the team had won, but they were also well equipped to handle any trouble. Their security as tenants, and their livelihood, however, depended not only on their own popularity but the success of the team, and should they wish to move club, even to a local rival, they obviously stood to lose custom. Their work load - as in the case of Hunslet's Albert Goldthorpe who had to miss the game at Hull on Guy Fawkes Night 1893, and Bradford's Joe Richards, a *"beer retailer"* with two outlets who requested that the Yorkshire committee should not pick him until after the busy Christmas period - very occasionally meant that they

Wakefield Trinity, Yorkshire Rugby Union Cup winners 1879. *From left to right – Back Row:* A. Hirst, W. Jackson, B. Longbottom, T. O. Bennett, Bell (Umpire), J. Longbottom. *Middle Row:* B. Kilner, W. Ellis, J. Whitehead (Seated). H. Pickersgill, A. Hayley (Captain), G. Steel, H. Hayley, J. W. Kilner, T. Parry, C. E. Bartram. *Front Row:* J. Leach (Secretary), C. T. Baldwin. Trinity are known to have paid their players broken-time as early as the 1881/82 season.

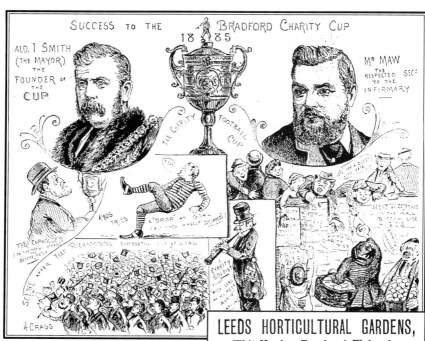

Scenes at the inaugural Bradford Charity Cup final, which was refereed by Reverend Marshall (see page 32).

It was due to such summer rugby competitions (this one took place during May, 1883) that "closed-time" was introduced in 1889.

74

Westmoreland club, Kendal Hornets, the 9-a-side champions of 1888. Seven of this side migrated to senior clubs in Lancashire and Yorkshire. *From left to right – Standing:* J. Allen, J. Armstrong, G. Battersby, R. C. Beard, J. Berry. *Seated:* W. Cross, W. J. Walker, J. Wilkinson, E. Wilson.

David and Evan James, Swansea's international half-backs, who were professionalised following their transfer to Broughton Rangers in 1892.

Scenes at Cardigan Fields, Leeds, on the occasion of Batley's victory in the 1885 Yorkshire Cup final.

C. E. Bartram, the first rugby player to be professionalised in connection with a testimonial, pictured on his 70th birthday, 7 July, 1926, when coaching Loretto School, Scotland.

A. N. "Monkey" Hornby (left), pictured with his Manchester and England colleague William H. Hunt.

Arthur Shrewsbury's tourists pictured prior to an Australian Rules game on 25 June, 1888. Shrewsbury is stood fourth from the left, and Robert Seddon is standing on the far right.

Andrew Stoddart (Blackheath), who captained the 1888 tourists, following the death of Robert Seddon.

"Dickie" Lockwood, who was questioned by Reverend Marshall over his move from Dewsbury to Heckmondwike (see page 115).

Yorkshire, the county champions, v. England, 23 February, 1889. *From left to right – Back Row:* W. Sykes, M. Newsome (President), J. Toothill, F. W. Lowrie, G. Jacketts, J. A. Miller (Hon. Secretary), H. Wilkinson. *Middle Row:* W. Stadden, R. E. Lockwood, F. Bonsor (Captain), H. Bedford, J. H. Jones, E. Holmes. *Front Row:* J. Dodd, J. W. Sutcliffe, A. L. Brooke, D. Jowett.

The scene at Fartown, Huddersfield, in 1891, when a crowd of 23,270 watched the Roses match in appalling weather.

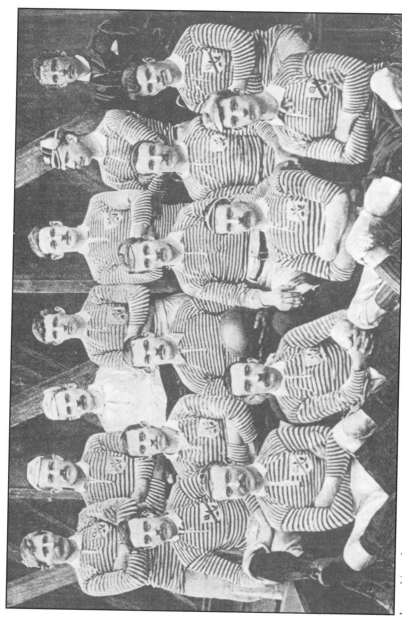

Lancashire, the county champions, v. England, 18 April, 1891. *From left to right – Back Row:* T. Craven, T. Rothwell, J. Berry, W. McCutcheon, J. Pyke, T. Kent, J. Strang. *Middle Row:* E. H. Flower, T. Whittaker, J. Valentine (Capt.), W. Atkinson, T. Melladew, T. Coop. *Front Row:* E. Bullough, D. Gwynn, W. Cross, R. P. Wilson.

County champions, Yorkshire, v. England at Headingley, 20 February, 1892.

The 'derby' clash with Huddersfield and Halifax at Fartown's newly improved ground (circa 1892). The line-out was still a feature of Northern Union rugby until it was abolished at the A.G.M. of 1897.

Halifax's J. P. Clowes, who was professionalised in 1888 for receiving a clothing allowance in connection with the first overseas rugby tour from Britain.

William "Buller" Stadden, Cardiff's international half-back, who joined Dewsbury in 1886.

H. W. T. Garnett, Yorkshire's first-ever President of the Rugby Union, who spoke in favour of broken-time.

Arthur "Sandy" Bairstow, who fell foul of the Rugby Union's rules related to professional cricketers.

William Cail, President of the Rugby Union in 1893.

Rowland Hill, Secretary of the Rugby Union.

James Miller, mover of the broken-time resolution.

Rev. Frank Marshall.

John Payne, Lancashire Secretary in 1893.

Dr. Arthur Budd, an arch opponent of broken-time.

F. I. Currey, who chaired the meetings, which were held to arrange the proxy voting against the broken-time proposal.

Mark Newsome, the seconder of Yorkshire's broken-time proposal.

Reverend Marshall caricatured as a certain Mrs Partington, who apparently endeavoured to sweep back the Atlantic with a broom.

were unable to get time off.  Nonetheless, being self-employed and able to work licensing hours certainly gave them advantages over most other working-class players.  Despite this relative freedom, however, rugby-playing landlords were certainly not always immune from the coercion of the rugby authorities.

Even though rugby union was ostensibly amateur, northern players were invariably placed in a dilemma due to the conflicts between their clubs and the county and national selections committees who were also demanding of their services.  As the game took on the characteristics of a semi-professional sport in the north, the players appear to have suffered much greater coercion than their southern counterparts.  It is unlikely, because of the nature of the game in the south and the Universities, that the above transfer restrictions and coercion equally affected those who might be termed *"gentlemen amateurs"*.

In February, 1893, for example, four Blackheathens opted to play for their own club against Bradford rather than the Rest of England side which faced Yorkshire at Fartown.  Following this game it was argued:

*Stoddart, Hubbard, Allport, and Lohden would ordinarily have been playing at Huddersfield, and some hard things were said about their conduct by the members of the Rugby Union committee.  A player remains his own master in southern football, whereas the Tykes are forced to make club interests subservient. Blackheath have set a bad example, and the Union countenanced it by agreeing to leave certain names off their "Rest" selection.  What would be said if Bradford's men decided by way of retaliation to stop at home next Saturday?* [25]

The latter point refers to the international against Scotland at Headingley, when, despite his disloyalty to the Rugby Union the previous week, Andrew Stoddart was still given the England captaincy.  In contrast, if a player in the north was chosen for his county, yet unable to travel because of Saturday morning work commitments, he was invariably banned from playing locally in the afternoon.  This also applied at international level, as in 1890 it was said by *The Yorkshireman*:

*One need not go back very far for examples of the restraints imposed on Yorkshire footballers, the recent England v. Scotland match (1 March, 1890) furnishing a remarkable instance...certain amateur sportsmen were ordered to play football at Edinburgh or remain in enforced idleness at home.. There is something radically wrong about this coercion business.*

Radically wrong it may have been, but it was obviously a long-standing practice.  After Halifax retained the services of J. Dodd and A. Wood, who had been chosen for Yorkshire's game against Midland Counties in 1882, the county threatened not to select players from offending clubs in future.  This worked for a time but in 1884 Bradford compelled their players to make a tour of the south, rather than play in the Roses match.

The county committee's authority in future was to be inflicted through expelling recalcitrant clubs from the Yorkshire Cup.[26]

Similar coercion also existed in Durham. Fred Alderson joined Hartlepool Rovers in September, 1889, at which time he was a native Northumberland player. The Durham county committee, however, asked him to captain their team, and, by way of persuasion, at the same time passed a resolution: *"That any player qualified and refusing to play for the county would not be allowed to participate in the Senior Cup Competition."* [27] Alderson had no wish to abandon Northumberland, but in fairness to Hartlepool he accepted the captaincy of Durham.

Naturally, employers and club patrons who may well have sponsored a player's transfer were also able to exert considerable pressure on him, to the point of apparently sacking a player because he requested a change of club. One known case, in 1891, was R. Earnshaw, a player with one of the junior clubs in Huddersfield, who alleged that he lost his job, which was subsequently taken over by another recruit to the side, after he requested a transfer to the town's senior club: *"One hears a great deal of the iniquities of the veiled professional,* wrote *The Yorkshireman, "but what about the tyranny of selfish "amateurs" who interest themselves in the engineering of their own pet clubs? We know the case of a young and brilliant player who was expected to go forward in the football world, who has during the past been told by his employer that he would have to play with a certain club or take the order of the "sack". Is there no remedy for such tyranny as this? When will honest professionalism begin?"*

There were also obvious problems for working-class players who could not get time off work. There are instances, such as with Bradford's Harry Noble in 1890, whereby working-class players lost the opportunity of being selected for the county, simply by being unable to break time in order to play in the mid-week trials. Saturday morning work, of course, also created many problems. Yorkshire forward Harry Wilkinson, a pattern dyer, could not make the journey to Northumberland in November, 1889 because the train left shortly after 9 a.m. Because of the county ruling Wilkinson was not permitted to play for Halifax, although finishing work at noon would have allowed him to do so.

Shortly after the broken-time meeting, however, it was argued that:

*"Broken-time of popular players is not all what it is made out to be. The employer of labour who gives noted footballers work does so with his eyes wide open. In nine cases out of ten he is a devoted follower of the sport, and makes no more trouble about letting-off than he did with the engagement of the men. As regards the anti-football type of employer, we believe that he is too good a hater to have players working for him at all. It strikes us that Mr Miller is seeking to*

90

*legislate for a class that has very little to complain about.*[28]

Certainly it was quite remarkable how working-class players were able to break time in order to take part in their county fixtures and particularly on club tours. At the Cumberland AGM in May, 1893, for example, it was reported that the county side had travelled over 2,000 miles to compete in their eight matches. They would normally have had either to travel on Fridays or very early Saturday, and on two occasions had been away from home for five consecutive days.[29] It was said that only rail and hotel expenses had been paid to the players, but was this possible without working men having a sympathetic employer, and equally understanding club and county officials? This rhetorical question is answered by *"Wag"* who informs us that:

*I come across a good many of these footballers, some of whom earn a pound a week, and have a wife and family to keep. If the incidentals of football were added to the home expenses, I fancy the Sunday dinner would frequently have to figure in the imagination, but happily the Yorkshire Rugby Union is spared the disgrace of indirectly bringing poverty and desolation to the hearth of the unfortunate half or three-quarter back, as the case may be, for I am credibly informed the latter is found in the enjoyment of "home comforts"...and is never without "spending brass" when abroad.*[30]

Evidence given of the Leeds Parish Church's tour in 1887 (see chapter six), and the fact that several clubs in Yorkshire are known to have threatened strike action or had other disagreements over tour expenses, would also confirm this. As well as being one of the perks of the season for the players and officials, touring, which commenced in the early 1880s, fulfilled an important function in popularising the game. In 1882/3, for example, Hull travelled over 1,700 miles to fulfil their dozen or so away matches, including a tour of the south in March. According to the club minutes, the players had their rail fares paid (less one shilling) and each received a 30 shillings allowance, out of which they had to pay their own bed and breakfast which apparently cost five shillings a night. Following Barron Kilner's international debut against Ireland in 1880, Wakefield Trinity started to tour the Emerald Isle. The 1883/4 tour cost the club £123 whilst players' allowances that season, including the tour, were said to be £35. Trinity also toured Wales in October, 1884, departing on a Tuesday morning, and playing Cardiff, Newport, and Swansea in successive days before arriving home in the early hours of Saturday. Welsh clubs soon reciprocated the arrangement, with, for example, Llanelli touring the north in December, 1884.[31]

The following Easter Dewsbury were met by a band at Llanelli station and were marched to their hotel amidst scenes of great enthusiasm. The

Welsh crowds were not to know, however, that this was merely a scratch side which the *"Shoddymen"* had sent, due to a strike by most of Dewsbury's first team, including their captain. Unable to dictate their terms to the committee, thirteen of the first fifteen refused to travel and they were replaced by *"old players and auxiliaries."* A similar disagreement, in October, 1890, saw Leeds' six-day tour to Bristol and Wales delayed due to the players apparently refusing to pay a portion of their expenses. In this case the penny-pinching officials, who had recently passed a resolution prohibiting players from having light refreshments at the club's expense after matches, climbed down, and the tour party headed off from Leeds 24 hours late.

Far from inconveniencing the players, therefore, tours were considered to be a highlight of the season, and leading clubs faced the problem of losing players if they were not prepared to meet the expense of such trips. When, for example, Wakefield Trinity, who had fallen on hard times in 1891, decided not to arrange a tour, it was asked, *"Where will next year's team come from if the committee break faith with the players?"* We need only look at the itinerary for Mannigham's tour in January, 1893, to realise the disappointment and envy that must have been felt by neighbouring club players who were denied such treats.

Manningham's 35-strong party were to leave Bradford on Friday morning, stopping in Birmingham for dinner, and arriving in Plymouth in time for supper. On Saturday, after visiting Plymouth Hoe in the morning, they were to meet Devonport Albion in the afternoon, following which they were to journey to their hotel at Torquay. Sunday was to be spent with the party being taken in two four-in-hand drags to Teignmouth, and after playing Torquay on Monday, they were to start the return leg of their journey the following morning. After lunching in Bristol for about three hours they were scheduled to arrive in Bradford late that Tuesday evening. This tour therefore entailed the loss of three and a half working days.

It is unlikely, if we take Alderson's comments over match expenses at Blackheath as an example, that there was any income to be made by *"gentlemen amateurs"* from ordinary club fixtures in the London area. They almost certainly did benefit, however, from their all-expenses paid tours of the north. The earliest touring side to Lancashire and Yorkshire appears to have been by the famous combined club Fettes-Lorretto, which was formed in 1881/2 following successful cricket tours to Yorkshire by the respective college cricket teams. They were captained by the legendary A. R. Don Wauchope, who, for one game in the north in 1893 played under the name of *"Hamilton"*. From December, 1881 until January, 1888 this student side won all but three of their games, namely, the draw against Edinburgh Academicals in 1884, and defeats by Bradford in 1886 and 1888. Loretto's headmaster, the puritanical H. H. Almond, rejoiced that the Rugby Union's opposition to broken-time prevented the game from becoming, "*a byword for money-grabbing, tricks, sensational displays and utter rottenness*", and a Fettes-Loretto club rule even went so far as to prevent members from accepting invitations to football dinners.[32]

Such high moral standards, however, did not prevent this college club side from having their expenses paid when on tour and taking a share of gate receipts. This certainly applied against Bradford, who also granted other visiting sides a 25% share of the gate and an allowance for expenses. According to Bradford's accounts for 1887/8, for example, Fettes-Lorretto received £37/10s as their share of the gate, and during that same season Bradford also paid out £30 each to Guys (who would have received this sum even had the game been cancelled) and Edinburgh Institute, £27 to London Scottish, £20 to Oxford University, and £12/10s to Richmond. The largest amount (£56/15s), however, was met for the visit of Blackheath, who, from their first visit to Yorkshire in 1886, had always received a quarter of the gate against Bradford. On the other hand, most, if not all, of the above tours by northern clubs, were met out of their own club funds. Bradford, for example, paid out £267 for their two tours in 1890/1 and never received any income when visiting Blackheath, despite the fact that this fixture invariably gave "*The Heathens*" one of their best gates of the season.

Later Bradford also extended this hospitality to the Barbarians, a club which was originally composed mostly of Blackheathians and which had been formed during W. P. "*Tottie*" Carpmael side's tour of Yorkshire and visit to the city in April, 1890. As the Southern Nomads, as Carpmael's side once called themselves, only played Wakefield Trinity and Huddersfield on this occasion, the Park Avenue side certainly did not pay for the famous oyster supper at Leuchter's Restaurant or the accommodation at the Alexandra Hotel.[33] However, the Barbarians, from their first visit to Bradford on 29 December, 1890, two days after their inaugural game against Hartlepool Rovers when they had ten internationals in the side, were presumably placed on similar terms to these other "*gentlemen*" touring sides.

Commenting on these arrangements, and the superior attitude of southerners to the broken-time proposal, one Yorkshire newspaper had this to say about their amateur credentials:

*Yet these very men who today are assuming such a position are of the self-same class as those who, when they have come north in the past have demanded payment of a considerable sum of money from clubs in this district....Did not these payments constitute professionalism quite as much as payment for broken-time would? Was not the money paid for the services of the men who travelled north? And did not the players receive a portion of it, if not in solid cash, in the form of hotel expenses etc. Why should a party of players, simply because they can afford to take a week's holiday in the winter, organise a tour and demand so much for each game played, in order that the outing might cost them nothing? Is there no "bastard amateurism" about this? They have had no scruples about taking for their personal expenses the funds of working men's clubs, but directly the latter suggest a system which shall place their players on a level with these professing puritans it is professionalism and illegal.* [34]

The Bradford committee may well have been thinking along these lines when they wrote to Blackheath during February, 1893, requesting that in future they should meet their own expenses, and that, whilst in London, Bradford should receive the same financial treatment accorded to *"The Club"* on their visits north. Blackheath subsequently communicated the fact that their committee had come to the conclusion that future fixtures with Bradford should be cancelled, *"owing to the style of play now adopted by the Bradford team."* [35] Greatly annoyed by this inference, Bradford then retaliated by cancelling the Easter fixture with the Barbarians on 9 April, 1893, most of the side still being composed of Blackheath players. Whatever reason Blackheath had for severing the fixture the Yorkshire press were unanimous in condemning their action.

*The Yorkshire Post,* whilst regretting that such a major fixture should be so abruptly ended, had this to say about Blackheath's *"spirit of lofty superiority":*

*(Blackheath) have no claim or fame left entitling them to lecture anyone, and their action in doing so is treated more as that of a presumptuous schoolboy than as that of men of the world and good sportsmen. Southerners can no longer charm the northern multitude by their "style" and the fact that Bradford in their nine home Senior Competition matches this season have taken £1,500 is a proof of the direction in which the popular taste lies. Such popular taste is an unerring guide to the genuineness of ability and "style". People will not patronise that which is not worth seeing.* [36]

*The Bradford Observer* also expressed similar sentiments in commenting:

*The rupture between Blackheath and Bradford is not very surprising when all the circumstances are considered. The fixture had ceased to attract at Park Avenue in anything like the old degree, and the Bradford committee are not the people to keep up a connection for the mere fun of the thing. Formerly it paid to have Blackheath down and to subsidise them freely, whereas Halifax or Hunslet is now a far better draw, and Bradford are quite justified in looking at the question from a business point of view. The suggestions about altering the terms emanated, of course, from Bradford, and we may take it that the cancelling was a natural consequence thereof. The Blackheathens can advance any reason they please. The fact remains that there was no thought of severing the connection until the financial side came to be discussed.*[37]

The first real rift between the north and south therefore took place six months prior to the crucial broken-time meeting, and, as Blackheath and Bradford failed to bury the hatchet prior to the latter becoming a founder member of the Northern Union, the above dispute must be considered to be something of a major landmark.

Another such landmark had occured in 1888, when the first overseas tour from these Isles had been undertaken. As we are about to see, it was the organisation of this tour and the nature of the players' expenses which were to present the Rugby Union with its first major confrontation since the 1886 legislation on professionalism. Should the reader still have any doubts regarding the extent of *"veiled professionalism"* during this period, these should be well and truly expelled by the end of the next chapter.

# Chapter Five
# **The Tour of 1888**

The first overseas rugby tour from the British Isles was organised by the Nottingham professional cricketers and sports goods business partners, Alfred Shaw and Arthur Shrewsbury. The Essex and England cricketer James Lillywhite, a cousin of the famous London sports outfitter, later failed to shoulder his share in this loss-making enterprise. Although it has since been absorbed into the game's official history, most likely due to Reverend Marshall having given it early credence in his authoritative book in 1892, at the time the tour was not sanctioned by the Rugby Union who professionalised one of the tourists for accepting a clothing allowance. No punitive action was taken by any of the home Unions against the rest of the tour party, although, from the evidence in Arthur Shrewsbury's own letters, it is more than likely that all these pioneers received this payment, and much more beside, on their nine month adventure Down Under.

In mid-1887 Arthur Shrewsbury, who was then at the pinnacle of his illustrious career as England's opening bat, had embarked on his second cricketing tour of Australia which was organised by himself and Lillywhite. Unfortunately, because of competition from G. F. Vernon's side, which also sailed out aboard the Orient steamer Iberia which landed in Adelaide on 25 October, 1887, Shrewsbury was soon aware that his cricketing enterprise, which finally lost £2,400, was destined for financial failure. In his correspondence with Alfred Shaw, who was left to manage the business back in Nottingham whilst he undertook the sales marketing in Australia and New Zealand, Shrewsbury appeared confident, however, that profits from their proposed football venture would offset the above cricket losses.[1]

This optimistic assessment appears to have been based, not so much on the rugby potential of the proposed tour, but the belief that Victorian (Australian) Rules football would be a real money-spinner. How realistic was it, however, to expect seasoned rugby players to attempt to master this totally alien game, even with the help in Australia of experienced coaches?

Neither partner appears to have been fully conversant with the Rugby Union's professional regulations, their approach to expenses and compensation payments to players obviously deriving from their cricketing backgrounds. The terminology which Shrewsbury used to describe the different class of player also came from this source. This is shown in correspondence on 23 September, 1887 when Shrewsbury advised Shaw: *"Even when you hear from us to engage the players keep it secret until you have fastened four or five of the principal ones. I think the more amateurs the better it will be."* Also, during the rain interrupted match against New South Wales on 9 November, 1887, when Shrewsbury cabled the code word *"Affix"*, which meant that Shaw should immediately start recruiting players, he added:

*The question of amateur and professional players is not recognized so much in football as in cricket, at the same time amateurs give tone to the team and you may well be able to get them to come for their bare expenses. We want the best of players and a few Scotchmen in the team would I think be popular.*

Shrewsbury therefore equated an *"amateur"* rugby player to a Gentleman cricketer, and, likewise, a working-class rugby player to a professional cricketer. That is, the latter would require a salary or weekly wage. From Tamworth, during February, he asked Shaw to forward, *"all particulars of engagements of players. Salary, length of stay and all other details"*, whilst having agreed the use of several grounds at favourable rates, he had earlier warned Shaw that, *"Some difficulty may arise if the players require a large share of the takings."* Shrewsbury then hit on the idea of approaching three members of his own cricket side, W. Newham, George Brann and C. Aubrey Smith, the latter two who did actually stay for a time, together with Andrew Stoddart who was then in Melbourne with Vernon's side.

Not only would this save four passages to and from New Zealand (which cost 80 guineas for the round trip) but Shrewsbury believed that this class of player would give the tour the added *"tone"* and status, thereby encouraging other southern players to join. This seemed to have more bearing than the fact that Smith and Brann were more experienced at soccer than rugby. Although, when the latter announced that he feared that his suspect leg would not withstand the rigours of rugby, Shrewsbury was quick to inform Shaw, *"should he stay now it will have to be on our terms."* Stoddart, on the other hand, had both impeccable social and rugby credentials, and Shrewsbury rightly saw the England and Blackheath three-quarter as the linchpin of his tour plans.

Anxious to secure the advice and services of England's future captain, Shrewsbury therefore thought it wise to send Stoddart an unsolicited cheque for £50 (approximately £1,500 at today's prices) before the rugby tour commenced. There is nothing in Shrewsbury's letters to suggest that Stoddart returned this, and therefore we can perhaps safely assume that the future emergency tour captain accepted this substantial retainer. Indeed, during January, in a cable from Melbourne, he was clearly playing the role which had been asked of him, advising Shrewsbury that C. L. Jeffrey, his colleague at Blackheath, would make an excellent tourist and should be approached.[2] Later, Stoddart also recommended another friend, R. C. Triston, who was about to sail home from Melbourne, but who was prepared to stay behind and play, on condition that Shrewsbury paid his travelling expenses. Neither Jeffrey nor Triston, however, subsequently joined the tour party.

Shrewsbury clearly had visions of their biggest pay-day being against a Victorian representative side under Australian Rules football. However, the Victorian Football Association's (V.F.A.) refusal to sanction the playing of games against the tourists should have warned him against the futility of this proposed exercise. He cautioned Shaw, on 22 December, 1887 from the White Hart Hotel, Melbourne, to delay seeking the approval of the Rugby Union, lest a refusal at this stage might jeopardise matters:

*All the press here are dead against the V.F.A. and they are certain to give in very shortly so you see we don't wish you to apply to the English Rugby Union until absolutely obliged to do so for fear they might not grant it.*

In order to save money on expensive cables, Shrewsbury devised a number of code words, by which he and his business partner could communicate on the major issue of official recognition of their tour. *Sheriden* was to inform Shaw to obtain the support of the Rugby Union, following which approval, Shrewsbury believed, the V.F.A. would immediately grant their patronage; *Beal* meant that the Rugby Union would not grant their patronage, preferring to remain neutral as they had no power in the matter; and *Turner* inferred that the Rugby Union had officially recognised the tour.

The latter code name refers to Henry Turner, the future secretary at Trent Bridge, who was appointed as the tour's agent in England. From his home at Lucerne Villa, Wilford Lane, Loughborough Road, Nottingham, Turner sent out the following letter, dated 30 December, 1887, to a number of well-known players:

*It has been decided by Messrs Shaw, Shrewsbury and Lillywhite to take out a team of Rugby Union football players to Australia next March, returning in September. The grounds have been secured in all the principal places. The rules of the Victorian Association differ somewhat from Rugby Union, the number of players being twenty-a-side...The greater number of matches will be arranged against clubs playing the Rugby Union rules. Six or eight matches under*

*Victorian Rules will be played but these will not be until late in the tour, thereby giving every opportunity to the team of witnessing games played under these rules as well as practicising them. I am desired by Shaw, Shrewsbury and Lillywhite to ask if you will form one of the team, in which case I shall be happy on their behalf to communicate terms to you, which I am sure will prove satisfactory. P.S. If you know, amongst your circle of friends anyone whom you think would be likely to take the trip, I should esteem it a favour if you would kindly send me his name and address.. Should prefer international players, if possible.*[3]

Among those who declined the invitation were Bradford's backs Rawson Robertshaw and Fred Bonsor, Charles Sumner and J. H. Potter, both of Leeds St. John's, and Don Wauchope, the Scottish international back who then played for Edinburgh Wanderers.

Shrewsbury was receiving conflicting reports on how the proposed tour was being received in England, including the fact that some journals were predicting a financial disaster. He therefore urged Shaw, on 4 January, 1888, to *"get the patronage of the Football Association"*, a term used continually by Shrewsbury when referring to the Rugby Union, *"and likewise get the English press, especially the football journals on our side."* Unfortunately for Shrewsbury and Shaw, official recognition of the tour was not forthcoming from either of the governing bodies. On 13 January, 1888 the V.F.A. again refused Lillywhite's request, although, on hearing that their resolution did not affect the individual clubs, Shrewsbury was undaunted and later engaged John Lawlor and J. G. McShane, the former captain of the Fitzroy club in Melbourne, as player-coaches. He was certainly more concerned, however, by the fact that Rowland Hill in London had sent out the following statement:

*The Rugby Union Committee wish it to be known that in response to the request from the promoters to give their support and approval to the projected football tour to Australia they declined to do so. They do not consider it within their province to forbid players joining the undertaking but they feel it their duty to let gentlemen who may be thinking of going know that they must be careful in any arrangements made that they do not to transgress the laws for the prevention of professionalism. The committee will look with a jealous eye upon any infringement of such laws, and they desire specially to call attention to the fact that players must not be compensated for loss of time.*[4]

Having heard this news, on 18 January, at which time he was still unsure whether Shaw and Turner had actually managed to raise a team, Shrewsbury wrote:

*If the Rugby Union can get players to come out without paying them anything all the better for us. It would be much better if the Union would select the players. By what your previous letter stated I was prepared to see a cable to the effect that the Rugby Union would make all the arrangements.*

When the tour party was announced, however, amid reports that it had at last received official sanction, Rowland Hill wired Australia, on Wednesday, 28 February, 1888, that the Rugby Union had not changed their policy. Moreover, on 2 March he issued a circular, enclosing a copy of the *"Rules of Professionalism"*, to each member of the tour party.[5]

Some weeks earlier Shrewsbury had advised Shaw:

*You would have to get a nice outfit, especially made for them, something that would be good material and yet take them by storm out here. You could also have a monogram worked on the front of it.*

Shaw duly obliged by kitting the players out in an impressive red, white and blue hooped jersey, which, of course, was common practice at every club in the land and perfectly legal. Shrewsbury and Shaw, however, could hardly have realised that it was to be their generosity in providing clothing of a different kind which would lead to the banning of one of their players on the day before the tour party sailed.

Henry Turner had sent contracts to Halifax's 21-year old forward, J. P. Clowes, and three leading Dewsbury players, the English international three-quarter *"Dickie"* Lockwood, Angus Stuart, and *"Buller"* Stadden, and all but the latter actually signed to go on tour. Stadden, however, placed his agreement in the hands of his club committee, and, following Lockwood's subsequent withdrawal and the knowledge gained from Stuart that he had received, like Clowes, £15 for the above outfit and preliminary expenses, Dewsbury were thus able to ensnare Halifax, whom they were to meet in a Yorkshire Cup-tie at Crown Flatt. Dewsbury had not forgotten the incident in the 1883 semi-final when Halifax had successfully appealed and caused the tie to be replayed, and they were determined to wreak their revenge. Stuart was therefore left out of the side on 3 March, 1888, and, as Reverend Marshall so eloquently put it, *"Dewsbury entered into the contest in the delightful position of standing upon velvet. They might win but they could not lose".*[6]

Having lost the match Dewsbury then accused (under rule number 6 of the Yorkshire Challenge Cup) both Halifax and Clowes of professionalism. Subsequently, at the Yorkshire committee meeting, on Monday, 5 March, 1888, Clowes openly admitted having spent the money in buying clothing and other articles necessary for the tour, and the committee therefore passed the following resolutions:

*1) That J. P. Clowes, having received £15 from Mr Turner of Nottingham for an outfit in connection with a football tour in Australia, has thereby received money consideration for playing football, and, in the opinion of this committee, is a professional according to the rules adopted in October, 1886. 2) That the Halifax club have played Clowes in ignorance of his receipt of this money, and the committee therefore order the match to be replayed on Wednesday (24 March,*

*1888) on the Bradford ground.*

At the conclusion of the meeting James Miller, Yorkshire's secretary, sent Rowland Hill the following telegram:

*Important evidence re: Australian team. Clowes disqualified by our committee for professionalism. Send commission to sit in Leeds on Wednesday night before the team sail. Evidence most conclusive, written and admitted. An authoritative declaration of the status of the team before starting most desirable. Am sending resolutions by post.*

The members of the inquiry, which sat in private at the Queens Hotel, Leeds, on Wednesday, 7 March, 1888, were J. MacLaren (Lancashire) chairman, Rowland Hill, secretary, F. J. Currey, past president, Arthur Budd (Blackheath), William Cail (Northumberland), T. M. Swinburne (Durham), and H. W. T. Garnett, A. B. Perkins and Mark Newsome from Yorkshire. Reverend Marshall, Gilbert Harrison and James Miller, the latter who placed the case before the committee, were also present during the hearing of the evidence. After examining both Stadden and Lockwood, and after deliberating for a considerable time the commission passed the following resolution:

*The Rugby Football Union has decided, on the evidence before them, that J. P. Clowes is a professional within the meaning of the laws. On the same evidence they have formed a very strong opinion that others composing the Australian team have also infringed those laws, and they will require from them such explanations as they may think fit on their return to England.*[7]

One question which remains unanswered is whether or not Lockwood and Stadden were required to implicate their colleague Stuart, who had apparently admitted to Stadden that he had also received the same clothing and preliminary expense allowance. Frank Marshall was certainly aware of this as he documented it later, but whether he gained this information at the above inquiry remains a mystery. Angus Stuart remained in New Zealand after the tour and later represented Wellington and Marlborough. He was also the veteran of the New Zealand side which toured Australia in 1893.[8] He returned to Dewsbury, long after the Clowes affair had died down, coaching the Dewsbury Northern Union club in 1902.

On the same night, the tour party had been entertained by the promoters, with the chief guest being Lord Newark, and the following day they embarked for New Zealand. In spite of the Rugby Union's decision, Clowes still accompanied the team, although Shaw stated that he would not take part in any of the matches, and this appears to be borne out by the available evidence. Clowes did, however, seek to have his ban lifted and sent the following letter, dated 8 March, from the *S.S. Kaikoura,* Plymouth, to Rowland Hill:

*As I have seen from the newspapers that the Rugby Union have endorsed the action of the Yorkshire County Committee...I wish to state that in doing this I acted in entire ignorance of the fact that I was in any way contravening the laws relating to professionalism. To prove the sincerity of my statement, I wish to offer to repay to Mr Turner, through you, the sum of £15 received by me from him and to ask the Rugby Union to reinstate me as an amateur. Your gracious consideration of this appeal will be deemed a great favour by your most obedient servant.*[9]

Whilst Clowes was left to ponder his fate, Halifax won the replay against Dewsbury more decisively. Ironically, it would be Mrs Mark Newsome, the wife of the Yorkshire and Dewsbury President, who would later present them with the Yorkshire Cup following their victory over Wakefield Trinity. Captain J. E. Bell, Halifax's secretary, waited until after the replay before making public his views on the affair. In so doing he revealed some previously unreported facts. In a letter to *The Yorkshire Post* on 19 March, 1888 he wrote:

*I am aware that the Rugby Union is not a legal tribunal, but surely...some regard should be had to the rules of evidence ... the witnesses being men who had themselves signed the agreement to proceed to Australia but had afterwards seen some reason for changing their minds. That being so was it fair that the case should have been decided in Clowes absence....or that one third of his judges should be men who had previously (passed)...a decision upon his case? The Yorkshire Committee admitted that they were quite unable to produce the slightest direct evidence against Clowes, who, conscious of his innocence, voluntarily offered the only evidence upon which he was convicted. (Rowland Hill's letter of the 2 March) in no way explains that any member of the Australian team receiving money from the organisers of the tour would be dealt with in the same manner as if they were receiving it from a member of their own club....In face of the facts that many University men and old players, and that the editor of such a paper as the "London Daily News" - 7th inst - should hold the same views upon this point as I do...is it to be wondered at that Clowes, a man probably not very well educated, should fail to interpret those rules in the same manner as the Rugby Union? What is the position of the Yorkshire Committee who selected men belonging to the Australian team to play for Yorkshire against Surrey at Huddersfield on the 30 February, and what is the position of the Rugby Union themselves, who selected Eagles as one of the international team and for which he received his cap, they knowing full well that he was going to Australia as one of the team, which was all that Halifax knew about Clowes?...It was also stated in evidence before the Yorkshire Committee (by a member of that same committee who recommended Clowes to Shaw) that Clowes informed Shaw that he was willing to go to Australia for his bare expenses in order to join his brother.*

Captain Bell concluded by asking, *"I wonder how many more applied to be taken on the same terms?".*

This was not too difficult a poser, given that the 20 men who climbed aboard the *S.S. Kaikoura* were mainly working-class northerners, predominantly from Lancashire and Yorkshire gate-taking clubs and the Scottish border club Hawick. There were at least two licensees, one self-employed player, and one professional cricketer in the squad, but one must assume that none of the players, with the possible exception of Smith, Brooks and Penketh, were of such independent means that they could have afforded to leave their jobs and families in England for 36 weeks without being well compensated. The party, which travelled out to meet Andrew Stoddart and his fellow cricketers Brann and Smith, was as follows.:

*Full-backs:* J. T. Haslam (Batley, Yorkshire and North), A. G. Paul (Swinton and Lancashire). *Three-quarters:* J. Anderton (Salford, Lancashire and North), Dr H. Brooks (Edinburgh University, Durham), H. C. Speakman (Runcorn, Cheshire). *Half-backs:* W. Bumby (Swinton, Lancashire), W. Burnett (Hawick), J. Nolan (Rochdale Hornets, Lancashire). *Forwards:* Tom Banks (Swinton, Lancashire), R. Burnett (Hawick), W. H. Eagles (Salford, Lancashire, England), T. Kent (Salford, Lancashire), A. J. Laing (Hawick), C. Mathers (Bramley, Yorkshire, North), A. P. Penketh (Blackheath and Kent Rovers, also lived at and captained Douglas, Isle of Man), R. L. Seddon (Swinton, Lancashire, England, captain), A. J. Stuart (Dewsbury, Yorkshire), W. H. Thomas (Cambridge University, Wales), S. Williams (Salford, Lancashire, North). *Umpire:* Dr John Smith (Cambridge University).

The side was captained by forward Robert L. Seddon who had co-founded Broughton Rangers in 1875. He was still with Rangers when he made his debut for England and played in all three internationals in 1887, but for the start of the 1887/8 season he transferred his allegiance to Swinton. Seddon, who was one of only four players who had decided not to get insured, clearly believed that risk-taking was part of life. The tour, however, would be marred by his drowning in the Hunter River at Maitland, New South Wales, on Monday afternoon, 15 August, 1888, the tragedy occuring when the boat which he was rowing overturned. Thereafter Andrew Stoddart took over the captaincy.

Together with Seddon, Swinton supplied four members of the squad, including the club captain and brilliant half-back, Walter Bumby, and county forward Tom Banks. The tall and powerful Swinton three-quarter and place-kicker Arthur Paul was the 24-year old son of an Army Officer who later became the Chief Constable of the Isle of Man. Born in Ireland and educated at Douglas (I.O.M.), he was a trained architect who had been a professional league right hand batsman and occasional wicket-keeper since 1882, firstly with Leeds Clarence and then Notts Castle, where Henry Turner was the secretary. After the tour Shrewsbury arranged for him to join the East Melbourne Club as a professional, although he did return to make his Lancashire debut in 1889, and in the late 1890s he kept goal for Blackburn Rovers.

Salford's contingent was made up of three of their leading forwards and the county three-quarter J. Anderton. Harry Eagles had been awarded his international cap in 1888, although, because of the international dispute he never played for his country. He was apparently the only player to play in all the 53 games of rugby and Australian Rules from 28 April until 2 October. This feat was almost matched by his club mate *"Sam"* Williams, who played in a mere 51 matches. Nottingham-born Thomas Kent, who joined Salford in 1887/8, would later make his international debut in 1891. One of the few self-employed players on the tour, he clearly felt it worthwhile to take part in this adventure and leave his business as a building contractor.

It was obviously worth it also for the only Welshman, and one of only four internationals in the squad, 22-year old William Henry Thomas, to leave his studies at Cambridge. Because of this break for the tour he apparently did not graduate until 1894, after which he became a schoolmaster.[10] He had won his first cap in 1885 whilst still a schoolboy at Llandovery College, and is described in *Fields of Praise* as, *"a young Goliath who spearheaded the Welsh pack"*. His form during the first New Zealand leg of the tour, however, certainly did not impress Arthur Shrewsbury, who rated him the worst player in the squad at that time. It is not known whether Thomas' form subsequently improved, although in 1891 better judges of rugby talent than Shrewsbury honoured him with the Welsh captaincy.

One player who certainly did impress Shrewsbury, at least on the field if not off it, was John Nolan, the Rochdale Hornets and county half-back. Clearly the character of the tour, Nolan finished as the leading try scorer with 16 from 19 games, scoring 10 of these in New Zealand. He was apparently offered £6 guineas a week to play Australian Rules, but in an interview suggested that ten times that amount would not stop him returning to his beloved Rochdale, where on his homecoming he was to receive a hero's welcome. He may well have regretted this decision, however, as a couple of years after his return he was sued for a substantial amount following a brawl at his public house in Oldham and also apparently lost his license.[11]

Following the withdrawal of Lockwood, Yorkshire's representation consisted of only three players, with one of those an exiled Scotsman, Angus Stuart of Dewsbury. Like so many of Yorkshire's county forwards

104

in this period, Charles Mathers, the Bramley captain and one of the club's founder members, had started life as a three-quarter. From about 1883, however, he had started to earn his reputation as a try-scoring forward, in which position, from 1884 until 1887, he made 14 appearances for Yorkshire. At the time of the tour Mathers, who was then 28 years of age, was the licencee of the New Inn, Bramley.

Batley's 24-year old Yorkshire full-back and winger, Tom Haslam, had starred in Batley's 1885 Cup-winning side. Prior to leaving he was presented with £15, with which he bought a gold Albert valued £6 and various items of clothing. At the presentation he said that he had been advised to seek a warmer climate due to the poor state of his health, and, being a bachelor with no ties, would have been foolish to have turned down the opportunity of touring.[12] Despite Haslam using the tour as something of a convalescent holiday, Shrewsbury rated him highly. Admitting that his side was not strong enough to take on a full New Zealand representative side, Shrewsbury paid Haslam a glowing compliment: *"I wish you could have sent us some internationals, such as Bonsor, Robertshaw, Lockwood, Jeffries and others. Haslam is about the best man in the team and is playing a magnificent game. We want three or four more like him"*, Shrewsbury wrote, prior to contemplating a defeat at the hands of Auckland.

The senior member of the party was the 33-year old former Queens Park, Corinthians, Swifts and Scottish soccer international, Dr John Smith of Cambridge University. His primary duty was to act as umpire. Dr Brooks of Durham City apparently intended augmenting his income by reporting on the tour for a Newcastle paper, and Shrewsbury envisaged using these accounts to publish a book when the tour ended.

There were a number of other names mentioned in regard to the tour. K. B. Ferguson, a Hawick forward, was said to have signed papers to tour but obviously withdrew[13]; and Tom Scarborough the former Halifax player who had emigrated, offered his services for the whole tour. Shrewsbury told him (on 5 June, 1888) that he would not be needed in New Zealand but asked him to learn the Australian Rules. Although it is not known for sure whether he did actually join the tour, Scarborough certainly played for Melbourne against the New Zealand tourists (see below) before the latter set sail for England.

Shrewsbury was still not aware of the Clowes affair or whom he would be managing when he wrote from the Oxford Hotel, Sydney, on 14 March:

*I expected when they left England the names would have been cabled out, but such has not been done. I can tell you candidly I am pleased they (Smith and Brann) are going home (as) we are having to pay them £200 each for expenses.*

*The only thing we are afraid of is that should Stoddart hear they are not staying he will want to go home as well. However, he doesn't know about this yet and we sent him on a cheque for £50 a few days since which should bind him.*

The previous day Stoddart had earned his keep by watching a specially staged exhibition of Victorian Rules football by the Melbourne and Carlton clubs on the Melbourne Cricket Ground immediately following the Victoria versus England cricket match. This convinced him that his future colleagues would have little trouble adapting to the game. Stoddart's assessment, based, presumably, upon his own all-round sporting abilities, was, unfortunately, well off the mark. Despite the appointment of the Australian Rules coaches, Shrewsbury would later confide to Shaw that, *"In the Victorian game, I can play better than some of our players, who don't shape well at all and never will. The elder Burnett and Laing don't appear to have the slightest idea how to play."* And although they would later win several games against the weaker sides, it was obvious by the time they reached South Australia in June that it had been a folly to play under these foreign rules.

The travel-weary and portly tourists - they had consumed £68 worth of drinks aboard ship - disembarked at Port Chalmers on 23 April, 1888. The following day (from the Grand Hotel, Dunedin) Shrewsbury admitted to Shaw that they had got the players cheap, and gave his first reaction to the Rugby Union's ban on Clowes:

*It was a great pity you sent Clowes out here as he won't be able to play in a single match and we shall have all his expenses to pay. When he looked like being disqualified you should have obtained a substitute. We shall have to try and make some arrangement with him to come home, or only pay his bare expenses... He is a dead-head and of no use at all.*

Shrewsbury later confirmed that Clowes would definitely remain on the sidelines throughout the tour, *"Clowes will not be played in any match unless you get the Union to cancel his disqualification"*, he wrote on 30 April, 1888. Shrewsbury was aggrieved that the Rugby Union, who appeared to have no jurisdiction over whether Clowes played Australian Rules, had not been approached on this point by Turner. The Halifax man appears to have spent more time with his brother than he did with the tour party and missed the boat on the return journey.

Shrewsbury enthused in the same letter, dated 24 April, 1888:

*They are working the excitement up admirably and expect 10,000 people to be present at the first game. At most of the New Zealand places we get 80% of the gross, the other side paying all expenses. Our fellows are having a rare time of it. They propose to drive them in a drag and four to all the country places where the scenery is worth a visit and they have free access to the rinks and places of entertainment and amusement. They were also entertained at Hobart by the*

Mayor and Corporation and toasted in champagne. They are delighted with the trip so far.

In a letter to his brother, Tom Haslam remarked on the concerts after every meal and the singing of Nolan and Speakman. Just how much the players over indulged themselves is perhaps indicated by the fact that *"Sam"* Williams, although playing in nearly all the games, still managed to add two stone to his slender 10 stone frame during the course of the tour!

We have already seen that Andrew Stoddart was paid a substantial retainer, and there is additional proof that payments, over and above legitimate hotel and travel expenses, were paid to other members of the squad. This is to be found in a letter written by Shrewsbury on 22 June. Shaw and Turner had promised the players that they would be home by the beginning of October, which was six weeks too early for Shrewsbury who re-negotiated their contracts in order to allow him to go into Queensland. This is what Shrewsbury wrote to Shaw from the White Hart Hotel, Melbourne:

*You must send Anderton's pay to his mother or whoever it is, a month extra, on account of him staying out longer. I will let you know whether to do the same with Nolan's people later on. It all depends how he behaves himself. Thomas, I see by the book, was to have £3 a week. Now if we were to give him £3 per week for the extra six weeks he stayed he will be having £18 for the extra time, whereas the other men are staying for nothing except Anderton. Originally Thomas was to have £90. If the thirty weeks he agreed to stay was divided into £90 for convenience sake, so as to arrive at what the amount would come to per week, then he won't be entitled to any extra money. If on the other hand you agreed to pay him £3 per week from the time he left home until his return, then we shall have to pay him the extra £18.*

In effect, therefore, the players were paid broken-time. The fact that the majority of the tour party were apparently willing to forgo such payments, during these extra six weeks, would appear to indicate that they were well satisfied with the pay and allowances already received.

In respect of other expenses, the so-called amateur cricketers, Brann and Smith were apparently a bad influence on the rest of the squad. *"I am pleased both went home,"* Shrewsbury told Shaw on 3 June from Sydney, *"as they ran our cricket expenses up frightfully which they also do (sic) in football and what is more set the example to the rest of the players."* In his reply in September, 1894 to Mrs Lillywhite, in which he refers to her late husband's mismanagement and dishonesty, Shrewsbury wrote, *"He allowed one of the footballers to overdraw to the extent of £60 or £70, knowing, as in the case of the money I lent him, that he was not in a position to pay one penny of it back."* Who this player was we shall perhaps never know, although

107

all the pointers lead to this *"amateur"* cricketing fraternity.

Shrewsbury calculated the total cost of the rugby tour to be in the region of £6,000, but he told Shaw, *"Of course, we tell everyone it will cost £8,000 or £9,000 and you may tell them even more."* In order to recoup some of this large outlay, at the early stage of his rugby tour Shrewsbury had been working on two ambitious plans. The first was to return via America, where he hoped he could make another £500, and thus emulate his world cricket tour of 1881/2. All but the three Hawick players agreed to this proposal and there must have been general disappointment when this tour was cancelled. Shrewsbury also had the idea to bring back the first New Zealand side, this time with the blessing of the Rugby Union, and had hoped to get 75-80% of the gross takings from such a venture.

Unfortunately for Shrewsbury this also had to be abandoned after he learned of a similar project that was being arranged by Joe Warbrick, a Maori three-quarter who had been in the first New Zealand side to tour New South Wales in 1884. Warbrick's main backers were to be J. R. Scott and Thomas Eyton, a wealthy expatriate who had lived most of his life at Blackheath. It would seem, however, that there were other business interests involved from the outset. There was no hiding Shrewsbury's bitterness, having heard that the Rugby Union had offered no objection to the tour (later they would agree to arrange the fixtures), when he wrote to Turner on 30 April from Dunedin:

*I am afraid we shall not be able to bring a New Zealand team home for next season, as the Maories got the start on us. They were only organised to play a series of matches in New Zealand. The thought would never have entered his (Warbrick's) head had we not been out here. I think it is a kind of company different people having shares in it. We wanted to play them a match but they were afraid of being licked. I see by cable the English Rugby Union have given them their patronage. I want to know whether these men are not professionals as when their trip is over and they find they have a balance in hand this will be divided amongst the players. As they are certain to have a balance at the end of the trip then it is a certainty they are being paid for their services.*

Whilst at Christchurch in May Shrewsbury had befriended one of these prospective backers, a Scotsman named Brown who had been willing to invest £400. He later withdrew, however, when Warbrick would not agree to his conditions. Most of the following information from Shrewsbury would appear to have been gleaned from Brown. *"Talk about speculation,"* Shrewsbury wrote, *"his is one with a vengeance and for the Union at home to give their support to it after refusing us, is a clincher. But I should imagine they will want to know something more about before the matches are arranged. They are wanting 75-80% of the gross takings. These men are professionals hundred to one more than Clowes and all of them I believe have arranged the terms to be paid them.*

On 9 September, from the Imperial Hotel, Auckland, Shrewsbury was able to confirm, what he understood to be, the terms which the team had accepted:

*The Maori team are coming over on the following conditions, viz J. R. Scott, a publican and betting man, who resides in Gisbourne, is finding the capital and takes 50% of the net profit. Joe Warbrick, the captain of the team, takes 25% net profit and the remaining 25% is to be equally divided amongst the rest of the team. So I should imagine that the team won't get much. If this is not professionalism and a speculation I don't know what is. The above you can take as being reliable.*

However, this was not the picture painted by the tour managers of the New Zealand Native Football Representatives, which was the correct title for a squad which comprised, *"six full blooded Maoris, 15 half-castes and four pure Europeans"*. The day after they played their first game against Surrey on 3 October, 1888, the Rugby Union AGM was read a letter from Thomas Eyton, the treasurer/joint manager, in which he stated:

*I wish to say that we are prepared to submit our accounts for inspection should you desire it at any time for the purpose of making it plain that no member of the team has received or will receive any remuneration for his services beyond his bare travelling expenses.*[14]

The Rugby Union committee were satisfied with this promise, and Frank Marshall would later state, in connection with the above undertaking, *"That the tour was carried out on strictly amateur lines may be accepted from the fact that the Rugby Union practically had control of the finances..."* [15] It would seem, however, that in the next 25 weeks until the end of March, 1889, during which time they played a staggering 74 games, *("it was absolutely necessary for them to play extra matches in order to obtain the necessary funds to enable the tour to be a financial success,"* - Marshall), the New Zealand tourists were never asked to submit their books, cooked or otherwise, for inspection. The official line therefore contradicted Shrewsbury, but, nonetheless, his opinion regarding the purity of the New Zealand tourists was perhaps vindicated when Patrick Keough, a native of Warwickshire, was suspended by the Otago Union in 1891 for, *"acts of professionalism."*

But what fate awaited the English tourists who arrived home on 11 November? Surely the Rugby Union would now hold a professional inquiry, at which Andrew Stoddart and the rest of the tour party would at least be questioned as to whether they had received a similar clothing allowance to that which had professionalised Clowes? In Yorkshire its committee had recommended clubs not to play members of the tour until the Rugby Union had decided upon their amateur status. This treatment, however, contrasted sharply with the other county Unions and the Rugby Union itself, the latter selecting Stoddart to play with London against Oxford and Cambridge Universities. Salford were allowed to play their four tourists, and Durham allowed Dr Brooks to play for Durham City against Leeds Parish Church.

*"Suppose,"* argued *The Yorkshireman, "that Lancashire plays any of the Australian tourists against Yorkshire next Saturday - say Eagles - will the Yorkshire County Committee act up to the sound moral precepts that they are instilling into Yorkshire clubs and decline to meet a team consisting of these "suspects?"*

Such a dilemma never arose, however, as, on 15 November, 1888, the Rugby Union committee simply requested that each player should, *"attest a Statutory Declaration that they had not infringed the Union's regulations, and that the county committees be authorised to take any further steps they considered wise."* [16] This, of course, the players were only too pleased to do. The Scottish Rugby Union at least took the trouble to question the three Hawick tourists, but we are able to ascertain little from the minutes which state succinctly: *"Their assurances being satisfactory, the matter was dropped until such time as direct evidence might be adduced in support of any alleged professionalism".* [17] As for Clowes, after earlier refusing requests from Halifax to have him reinstated, the Rugby Union lifted his suspension on 22 November, 1888, and thereby closed the book on the whole affair. [18]

Some years later, however, Arthur Budd, who had been a member of the commission which had investigated Clowes in his absence, would express the opinion that the Rugby Union had been too lenient in whitewashing the tour party. In addressing the professional question in general he wrote:

*The first dusting was with the members of Shaw and Shrewsbury's team, who were asked to make a declaration of their own integrity. What reason was there in this? Will not a man who takes money behind your back be ready enough to swear anything before your face?* [19]

Budd, of course, was perfectly correct in his assessment of human frailties but it is highly unlikely that he also had in mind a fellow Blackheathan. It is almost certain, however, that Andrew Stoddart would have been the highest earner, as, by Shrewsbury's own admittance, the rugby players who were signed by Turner in England, came cheap. Having little idea of the going-rate for such tours they appear to have accepted salaries at about a quarter the size of those given to cricketers - that is, £200-250 for 21 weeks, as distinct from £90 for 30 weeks. [20] It is highly unlikely that an experienced cricket mercenary such as Stoddart would have been so naive as to accept these latter terms, particularly when he was expected to play such a leading part in the enterprise.

As for his own work in 1888, having forfeited a summer's cricket at the height of his career, Shrewsbury had to also shoulder part of the deficit of £800 from his football tour. These losses were due, in part, to the poor returns from many of the Australian Rules games, and the alleged fiddling of the gate receipts at some of the major rugby matches. They were also caused by the indifferent form show by the players, particularly against Auckland in the first leg of the tour, when Shrewsbury said that, *"We simply lost the match through our players not taking care of themselves, too much whisky and women"*. This placed Shrewsbury in a weak position in the return fixture and he had to accept only 25%, rather the original 40%, of the net gate. Bad weather also affected several major games, and an estimated £100 was lost due to cancelling a fixture following Seddon's death.

Referring to those first New Zealand tourists, Shrewsbury made the prediction that, *"They are sure to get many a licking at home (but) before many seasons have gone by a New Zealand team is certain to come over and a good one it will be"*. Although this assessment was not exactly accurate, in that Joe Warbrick's side managed to win 49 of their games, Shrewsbury, it seems, was anticipating the day when New Zealand rugby would become a trulyworld force. Unfortunately, however, having committed suicide on 19 May, 1903, when suffering from what he believed to be an incurable illness, Arthur Shrewsbury would not live to see the day that his prophesy would come true, in the form of Dave Gallaher's revolutionary 1905 All Blacks.

# Chapter Six
# Professional Inquiries prior to the 1893 Broken-Time Meeting

Shortly before Shrewsbury's pioneers began to make their way home and the first New Zealand tourists arrived under a similar suspicion of being rugby mercenaries, the game in England had seen the first case of a club being professionalised. Almost inevitably, this was in Yorkshire, as, prior to the broken-time meeting, most inquiries were instigated by this county. Until the 1890/1 season the Lancastrians showed a reluctance to acknowledge the problem, and it was only because of Reverend Marshall that Oldham were asked to justify their recruitment policy. So-called professionalism was patently not unique to Lancashire and Yorkshire. Tentative research has revealed that in Cumberland, Westmoreland, Durham, and Gloucester (a few months after the period currently under discussion) clubs fell foul of the professional regulations. We may perhaps surmise, therefore, that had Frank Marshall resided in any other part of the country several more cases might have been unearthed. Nonetheless, the chief prosecutor's success rate for gaining convictions was not over impressive.

In an interview in January, 1888, Reverend Marshall admitted that the regulations of 1886 had largely proved ineffective.[1] He believed that, although there had been no tangible proof, *"veiled professionalism"* mostly took the form of players being found work rather than them being paid for playing. *"The matter is a very difficult one to get at,"* he answered, *"and it won't be got at until some rule is made by which if a man changes his club he is bound to give his reasons for doing so. At present professionalism must be proved. If there is such a scheme as I suggest carried out it would enable the committee if they had a suspicion to stop men from playing, and the players would have to come before the committee with clean hands and prove themselves not guilty."* He ruled out the prospect of players having to have a residential quaiification, and his thinking at that time later resulted in his drafting of comprehensive transfer regulations which were approved in October, 1891.

In the meantime, the Yorkshire committee grappled with the

*"interminable transfer cases"* the best way they could. In February, 1889 they decreed that a player's transfer refusal should last until the end of the season, and all transfers after 1 December, 1889 had to come before the committee for approval. Furthermore, players who were granted their transfers after 1 February, 1891 were ruled ineligible for the Yorkshire Cup-ties.

Despite such transfer obstacles, which greatly affected the leading clubs' ability to build up an adequate reserve strength, there were very few players or clubs who were professionalised prior to September, 1893. Arthur Budd's estimate in 1895, that there had been only about a dozen such convictions, could not have been far short of the mark.[2] These, in effect, amounted to little more than the scapegoating of clubs and players who were unfortunate enough to have evidence brought against them. Before we examine most of the known cases (but excluding the testimonial cases which have been mentioned previously) it is perhaps necessary, therefore, to bear in mind the following opinion:

*The stock in trade of the modern professional prosecutor is the argument of suspicion. If carried to its legitimate conclusion this method - un-English, by the way - would hang half the football men in Yorkshire. The fact is incontrovertible that many scores, I might almost say hundreds, of modern players find it possible, and not only possible but necessary, to break through one or other of the hard and fast commandments which the framers of our modern Decalogue have laid down, and by which they are sought to be bound hand and foot....our legislators have adopted a standard of perfection which is tyrannical in its operation and absurd in its logic.*[3]

Given that this was a correct assessment, it was therefore understandable that the supporters of Leeds St. John's should feel aggrieved at being the first club in the country to be suspended.

On 1 October, 1888 the Yorkshire committee were satisfied with the allegations from Kirkstall that one of their leading players, the unemployed printer F. A. North, had been offered a job at Goodall & Suddick in consideration of him joining Leeds St. John's.[4] In the absence of James Miller, the St. John's President, whose duty, as county secretary, it should have been, Reverend Marshall was given the task of presenting the evidence to the Rugby Union commission, which met in Leeds on 18 October. Consequently, St. John's were suspended until 1 December, and North, although he was later permitted to join Holbeck, was refused permission to play with the future Headingley organisation. St. John's suspension also meant that six other Yorkshire clubs stood to lose their home fixtures against the premier Leeds club but, as we shall see, measures were later taken to appease such innocently-affected clubs.

The next suspension also involved a future Northern Union founder member in the form of Brighouse Rangers, which had been formed in 1880 by Henry Hirst Waller and a few of his ex-school mates from Silcoates College, Wakefield. His grandfather had been a partner in a company which introduced cotton spinning into the town and which owned the Low Moor Iron Company. After retiring from the game due to breaking four ribs against Wakefield Trinity, Henry Waller served on the Yorkshire committee and the Yorkshire Senior Competition, and after the split in rugby was elected as the Northern Union's first President.

One vigilant reporter had cryptically remarked during April, 1888, *"Isn't it strange that seven footballers are employed at one dyeing establishment in Brighouse!"* It therefore came as little surprise that the ambitious Rangers should be eventually accused of professionalism. The charge, which was heard by the Yorkshire committee on 12 November, 1888, was brought by Liversedge, who alleged that during May, 1888 Herbert Hartley, who at that time was in full employment as a stoker at Liversedge Colliery, had met with representatives of Brighouse Rangers and shortly afterwards obtained work at Richardson's silk spinning works. It was also alleged by William Fisher, a future captain of Yorkshire, that Hartley had admitted receiving £20 from Rangers' patrons.

Documentary evidence, which was produced in his defence, only went to prove that Hartley had left a better paid job, in order to work part-time. The Yorkshire committee therefore found both the player and the club guilty of professionalism, and Rangers were subsequently suspended by the Rugby Union until 26 December, 1888 and Hartley until the end of the season. At the end of his suspension, although he had kept wicket for Brighouse during the summer and had lived in the town for the previous eighteen months, Hartley was not allowed to transfer to Rangers.[5]

Not all cases were as clear cut as the above, and the committee were often charged with being inconsistent in refusing transfers and handing out suspensions. For example, the case against George Barratt, who was refused his transfer from Normanton to Castleford during December, 1888 and suspended up to and including the 1 February, 1889, produced no direct evidence of any material inducement, and, indeed, the Castleford club were totally exonerated.[6] Although the same could not be said in the case of Cleckheaton, who, during January, 1889, were successfully prosecuted by Low Moor (Bradford), the inducement was nothing more than a trouser length, which Cleckheaton claimed had been given as a prize for the player who attended most training sessions.[7]

Aggrieved at such inconsistancies and the effects which the

professional suspensions were having on innocent clubs, 48 Yorkshire clubs convened a special general meeting of the Yorkshire Rugby Union on 19 February, 1889. The outcome was that a resolution by Halifax's Captain Bell was withdrawn in favour of Reverend Marshall's amendment. This meant that guilty clubs were required in future to play the away matches, which had been cancelled, at the end of their suspension.[8]

Another milestone was the case of C. E. *"Teddy"* Bartram of Wakefield Trinty.[9] Principally, in that he was the first player to be banned for life from the game for professionalism, and also that his was the first instance of a player and his club being found guilty in connection with a testimonial. Bartram, who was a centre three-quarter in Trinity's great Cup sides of the 1880s, having captained them from 1883, also made 14 appearances for Yorkshire and played in three North-South matches from 1882-4. Despite this success he was never chosen for England, being described as, *"too professional for the southerners' liking"*. This was not only a reference to his ability to bend the playing rules but the suspicion that he was a kept man. It was following his retirement that his amateur status was officially questioned after allegations that Trinity had contributed towards his testimonial fund. The Yorkshire committee, which met on 15 and 19 July, 1889, finally decided that Bartram had received at least £50 from Trinity, both towards his testimonial and in the way of unpaid loans. Trinity were therefore suspended until 31 October, 1889, and Bartram, who continued his paid cricket career with North Leeds, was declared a rugby professional. To add insult to injury, Trinity's appeal was later dismissed and the £50 deposit, which Trinity forfeited, was put aside by the Rugby Union to help towards the costs of future inquiries.

The next case was notable for the fact that it involved three England internationals, the greatest wing three-quarter of the early 1890s, Richard E. Lockwood (ex-Dewsbury), Willie Jowett, and John W. Sutcliffe (both formerly of Bradford), with the sex-life of the latter directly contributing to his club being placed under scrutiny. Heckmondwike had seen a rapid rise in new trades during the previous three years, and with this industrial prosperity the rugby club were able to attract players of the highest calibre, Sutcliffe (a slop dyer), Jowett, and Noble all working at the same factory. *"Dickie"* Lockwood, on the other hand, had continued to work in Dewsbury as a woollen printer.

The *"football phenomenon"* Sutcliffe had been co-habiting with a Nancy Jubb and the case had resulted from her brother making allegations against the Heckmondwike centre three-quarter and captain. Not surprisingly, it was Reverend Marshall who was asking most of the questions at the Yorkshire committee meeting on 19 September, 1889.[10] Casting his mathematical and cynical mind over the club's figures from October, 1886, Frank Marshall queried the fact that during the whole of the 1888/9 season there had been only two gates over £20. Also, there were apparent discrepancies over insurance and refreshment payments to players, as well as hotel expenses whilst on tour. Nancy Jubb's brother, a hostile witness if ever there was one, alleged that Sutcliffe had told him that he received 10 shillings a week for playing with Heckmondwike. This, of course, was denied by the player, but other witnesses not only confirmed Jubb's evidence but stated that they had overheard one of Heckmondwike's vice-presidents admit to paying their players. After a long deliberation the committee passed the following resolutions:

*1) That the books of Heckmondwike are unreliable. 2) That it has been proved that cash received and paid to players has been omitted from the audited cash book. 3) That Rule 1 Section B of the Insurance Laws has been broken. 4) And by evidence brought against certain players the committee feel justified in continuing their inquiries. 5) Also that the Heckmondwike club is suspended sine die* (later terminated at 31 December, 1889).

Of the above players only Lockwood came in for further interrogation by Reverend Marshall, who based his case on the evidence of a former Dewsbury member, who had accused Lockwood of receiving 10 shillings a week and £1 for each of a number of exhibition games during his time at Dewsbury. It was not until January, 1890 that the case against Lockwood collapsed, when the Yorkshire committee finally expressed their, *"intense indignation at the pusillanimous conduct of the individual who, whilst not hesitating to make public the charges, has not the moral courage to support them."* [11]

Sutcliffe meanwhile had not been slow to cash in on his extraordinary footballing talent. The week following Heckmondwike's suspension - after training at Bolton with Noble, who was found to be unsuited to the other code - Sutcliffe signed professional forms with Bolton Wanderers. For his debut in the reserves against Accrington, Bolton decided to try their new acquisition at centre-forward, and for a while he appeared to have adapted quite well to his new role. When Sutcliffe managed to get in his first shot, however, his rugby instincts immediately took over, as he followed up and crash-tackled the goalkeeper head first into the mud - an incident which resulted in both sets of players, and the crowd, being convulsed with laughter. Nonetheless, by 1890, after a spell at full-back, Sutcliffe became Bolton's established goalkeeper, a position which most rugby commentators had earlier suggested would be his rightful position, bearing in mind his astonishing kicking skills. Moreover, between 1893 and 1903 he played for England on five occasions, never once being on the losing side.[12] Professional soccer was therefore one avenue open to the most highly talented of rugby players, but the Rugby Union would soon see to it that there was no way back.

There were also few loopholes left for those rugby players who were also gifted on the athletic track. At the Yorkshire meeting on 19 December, 1889, George Broadbent, a leading sprinter and Leeds Parish Church captain, was declared a professional following a sub-committee report which looked into his transfer from Holbeck in October, 1887. At the meeting referred to below, at which Broadbent's suspension was upheld, James Miller read out the details of the suspension at the request of the player. These were as follows:

*Broadbent left Holbeck because his testimonial was £15 and not £25; members of Holbeck paid his fees at Yorkshire College; he was paid for playing in a Cup-tie against Manningham; various inducements were made for him to join the club in October, 1887, namely that vice-presidents gave him a loan without interest to buy a shop in East Street where he would be assured of the custom of the club's followers; and he was employed as a "waiter" at the Scarborough Hotel on Saturdays and Sundays and his presence was advertised by the proprietor.*

During April, 1890 the Northern Counties Athletic Association confirmed the Yorkshire Rugby Union decision, which compelled Broadbent to run professionally in America.

The case against Leeds Parish Church had been heard on 20 January, 1890, when Reverend Marshall had questioned officials regarding grants to players whilst on the club's tour to Cheshire in April, 1887, and plumbing work on the new clubhouse which had been carried out by one of their players.[13] It was said by the club treasurer that the entries during April, 1887 were, *"those expenses that they deemed provident to spend upon the players in going about Liverpool and enjoying themselves."* The items included cigars, champagne, an oyster supper, a visit to the theatre, and a pleasure cruise on the Mersey, making the total cost of the tour £69. An entry for £37 on 30th April, 1887 for *"presents to the players"* had been crossed out and the word *"testimonials"* inserted. It was explained that these were rewards for success in the cup-ties: *"Some got suits of clothes, others watches. No money was given, the impression at the club was that it was legal to give presents but not money."* The committee drew attention to the rules which prohibited both gifts to players and work being undertaken by members of ones own club, and subsequently suspended Leeds Parish Church until February, 1890.

During this month the Rugby Union committee decided to delegate to county committees the various powers under the professional regulations, whilst also adopting the following resolution:

*a) Every testimonial to any member connected with a football club belonging to the Union is illegal, and both the giver and receiver shall be considered as infringing the laws of professionalism unless the presentation has been sanctioned by the county committee. b) No man who has been suspended or has contravened the regulations ...as regards to professionalism shall either play, umpire or referee without first obtaining the sanction of the Union committee. c) Any player registered as a professionalism under the rules of the F.A. is a professional within the meaning of the regulations of the Union with regards to professionalism.*[14]

These, of course, were as a direct result of the above cases in Yorkshire, as, apart from investigations into the running of the South East Lancashire Union, the Lancashire Rugby Union do not appear to have been greatly interested in such matters.

Then, in September, 1890, Mossley charged Werneth with enticing away A. Ashworth with the prospect of a better job, which resulted in the suspension of Werneth until 31 December, with the player suspended *sine die.*[15] A 3,000-name petition pleaded that the suspension should be allowed to end prematurely, in order that they could play Salterhebble with proceeds going to the Oldham Infirmary, but this was refused by the Lancashire committee which met on 23 October, 1890.

The main business at this meeting was the inquiry into Oldham, which followed a request, by the Yorkshire President, Reverend Marshall, that they should be asked to account for the appearance in their side of players from as far afield as Wales. Although no specific charges were made, Frank Marshall had apparently threatened to lay the matter before the Rugby Union but this was unnecessary as the Oldham representative immediately suggested an inquiry, in order to clear the club's name.[16]

Consequently, fourteen Oldham players and several club representatives, including Joseph Platt,[17] appeared at the Grand Hotel, Manchester, to face questioning from John Payne, the Lancashire secretary, and to have the club's books examined. The inquiry was held in camera but it was ascertained that the first to be called were Oldham's three Welshmen; half-back Thomas, and ex-Swansea backs, William (Billy) McCutcheon, a future international and a leading referee and administrator in the Northern Union, who made his debut on 8 December, 1888, and the club captain and international, Dai Gwynn, who arrived in Oldham during April, 1890. Most queries were apparently concerned with the reasons for the players' migrations, and the size of their past and present wages. John Nolan, who explained that his reason for leaving Rochdale was due to Hornets' supporters *"sodding him off the field"*, Pennington, James Hurst, Pendlebury, Bennett, and Rigby were also called, whilst the following Wednesday, 29 October,

1890, John Hurst was also examined over his move from Leigh.

When late that evening the resolution, *"That this committee, having heard all the available evidence, do not see any reason to take further action"*, was finally made known there was great rejoicing outside the local newspaper offices in Oldham, with many in the large crowd apparently expressing the wish that, *"...the Reverend gentleman should pay an early visit to the Watersheddings"*. Apart from sending him threatening letters, the opportunity to vent their feelings at the Yorkshire President came, as we have seen, when he attended the Roses match at Fallowfield.

What the general public were not aware of, however, was the fact that Frank Marshall continued to carry out further investigations into Oldham. This resulted in a sub-committee of the Rugby Union re-opening the case at the Grand Hotel, Manchester, on the morning of the Lancashire-Rest of England match at Whalley Range, on 18 April, 1891, when they passed the following resolution:

*The sub-committee are satisfied on the evidence laid before them, and on the examination of several witnesses, and of Nolan and Pennington themselves, that the charge of professionalism against the Oldham Club has never been substantiated. At the same time the sub-committee wish to state that they consider Mr(sic) Marshall was quite justified on the information brought to his notice in re-opening the inquiry.*[18]

Nonetheless, it would take more than Marshall's vigilance to stop the movement of rugby talent around the country, a trend which was aggravated due to the attractions which the north held for Welsh players, and the pressure on the leading gate-taking clubs to strengthen their sides.

The Yorkshire committee, on 9 November, 1891, held an inquiry into the transfer to Halifax of Cardiff Harlequins' centre-threequarter Bill Keepings. Keepings stated that he arrived in Halifax one late September evening and stayed at the hotel run by Jimmy Dodd, the Halifax captain. Next morning he found work as a *"holder up"* in the boiler-making trade in which he had been employed in Cardiff, and, having heard from Dodd that one of the Halifax backs was injured, was immediately selected to play against Rochdale Hornets. He denied that anyone from the Halifax club had first approached him, and, as Cardiff Harlequins had made no objection, his transfer was granted.[19]

It was not quite so simple, however, for the brilliant Swansea and Welsh international half-backs Evan and David James when they decided to take their crowd-pleasing act to the north in April, 1892. It was claimed by Swansea that both brothers, who were labourers in a copper works, had left the club after being refused match payments of 30 shillings a week, and they therefore referred the matter to the Welsh

Rugby Union, a body which appears to have had an ambivalent attitude towards the professional rules. At that Union's AGM in May, 1892, W. H. Gwynn (Swansea), said the professional rules were not only "*totally unnecessary*", but were also "*unsuitable to the game as played in Wales*". Their existence, he argued, did not alter the fact that, "*they had been constantly broken by the majority of the Welsh clubs and had never been enforced*".[20] This may account for the fact that, whilst bemoaning the loss of some of their best players to English clubs, and clearly wishing to frighten other prospective migrants, the Welsh Rugby Union nonetheless appear to have passed the buck over the James brothers to the English authorities.

Although they were originally bound for Huddersfield, both brothers were included in the West Hartlepool side which met Hartlepool Rovers in a charity match on 20 April, 1892, and the following Saturday they also played played against Harrogate. They later moved to Broughton Rangers, and the original inquiry by the Lancashire Union resulted in the "*exculpation both of the players and the club*".[21] The Lancashire Union, all along, were satisfied that, if any illegal transactions had taken place, they had been carried out on Welsh soil. However, following a further inquiry by the Rugby Union in October, 1892, both brothers were debarred from playing with Rangers and subsequently declared professionals. On appeal in February, 1893 this decision was upheld, whilst in early April, 1893, the Rugby Union committee adopted the report of its inquiry team which read:

"*...having heard the case against the Broughton Rangers F.C., whilst compelled by the evidence produced to give a verdict of "not proven", are firmly of the opinion that many of the circumstances closely connect members of the club with the migration of the brothers James and their subsequent manner of living in Lancashire, and that the further evidence fully confirms the previous decision - that the brothers James are professionals.*[22]

It was a curious case in which the players, who were later reinstated as amateurs in 1896, were professionalised in England, apparently on the basis that, "*the asking for a money payment constituted an act of professionalism equally as the acceptance of it*".[23] Broughton Rangers, on the other hand, were completely exonerated, although it seems, of course, that they were not entirely above suspicion.

Apart from the unfortunate Werneth, Lancashire clubs generally appear to have led a charmed life, certainly when compared to other northern counties. For example, on 7 March, 1892 Yorkshire suspended Normanton *sine die* for offering improper inducements to a Selby player, Huggins[24]; and the Durham County committee on 19 October, 1892, whilst severely censuring South Shields Y.M. Club for the lax manner of their book-keeping, also professionalised Joe Wheatley, Houghton's county forward, for breaking rule 2 (d) of the 1886 regulations.[25] Furthermore, on 3 November, 1892 the Rugby Union censured Westmoreland for granting permission to Kendal Hornets to play a benefit match for a player named Fawcett, and suspended a member of the club for three months[26]; whilst on 15 March, 1893, the Cumberland Union suspended J. Alderson of Whitehaven for a short period on the grounds that he had written to the above-mentioned South Shields club, promising to play for them if they would find him work, preferably in a public house. When the matter was referred to the Rugby Union, however, Alderson was declared a fully-fledged professional.[27] In that they were subsequently reinstated as amateurs, it is also known that in Yorkshire there were at least three other players, including former Thornes international three-quarter Harry Wigglesworth, who were professionalised at some stage in their careers. In contrast, it would appear from the evidence of present research that it was not until after the broken-time meeting that Lancashire clubs felt the full weight of the professional regulations.

In terms of the number of prosecutions, it clearly helped if there was one influential person in a county to whom informers could turn for help and guidance. This is confirmed by the fact that among Reverend Marshall's post on 29 October, 1892 was a letter, seeking his advice, from a Mr Hopkinson, the former secretary of the neighbouring Elland club. Subsequently, Hopkinson forwarded certain private books which he had kept whilst in office, and which Reverend Marshall believed were sufficient evidence to warrant a case being brought against Elland for falsifying payments to their players during the 1890/1 season. Sufficient, in fact, for him to immediately send a £10 deposit and bring the charges in the name of Almondbury Grammar School Football Club.[28] The case before the Yorkshire committee, at which Reverend Marshall was supported by his solicitor brother, commenced on 6 December, 1892 and, after two adjourned meetings the committee unanimously passed the following resolutions:

*1) That the charges formulated by the Almondbury Grammar School F.C. are not proven. 2) The Committee express their disapproval of the unsatisfactory, loose, and unbusinesslike way in which the books of the Elland Club have been kept and the accounts audited. 3) The Committee return the deposit, as although they do not consider the charge a frivolous one, they are sorry that Mr(sic) Marshall should have relied upon the sole testimony of Hopkinson.*

James Miller, the President, added that the evidence was of such a contradictory nature that they were compelled to reject it, although had Hopkinson's evidence been corroborated their verdict would have been different. He regretted that a stricter inquiry had not been made before bringing the case before the committee as, *"It was not only a taint and a charge against an individual club but affects and befouls the whole county in the eyes of the football world. There is a suspicion abroad,"* concluded Mr Miller, *"that football in Yorkshire is tainted with professionalism, and I think it cannot be denied that the recurrence of cases and inquiries such as we have concluded adds strength to this suspicion and makes Yorkshire regarded with no friendly eye by the other counties, as well as by Scotland, Ireland and Wales, while it also entails very great hardship on the representatives of Yorkshire who have to uphold the dignity of the county in other places."* [29]

One senses from Miller's remarks that Frank Marshall's efforts were not entirely appreciated. In fact, they amounted to a public rebuke from the man who would also clash with him at the broken-time meeting. As for Reverend Marshall's popularity in Elland, it is known, from the testimony of one of his pupils, that subsequent journeys through that neighbouring village, especially when going up the steep incline to Ainley Top, were fraught with extreme anxiety and danger - the youths of Elland appearing to obtain great pleasure from stoning and sodding the carriage, which carried the easily-recognisable Marshall and his boys as they cantered through on their way to Rishworth. [30] Matters did not quite reach that pitch at the Westminster Palace Hotel but, as we shall see, many of the Yorkshire delegates might well have welcomed the opportunity of aiming such blows at their pugnacious adversary.

# Chaper Seven
# **The Great Debate**

The need for broken-time was raised as early as the Lancashire AGM in 1886, and Captain Bell of Halifax also spoke in favour of the concession at Yorkshire's meeting during February, 1889, when he asked, *"Would it not be better to give compensation for loss of time to the working man, who enjoyed his football in the same way as the rich man, than to allow the evil professionalism which they all knew existed?"* [1] Immediately following James Miller's speech (see below) to the Yorkshire club secretaries in March, 1891, there were a number of other official pronouncements in support of his views, whilst Batley members actually passed a resolution in favour of broken-time at that year's AGM. Therefore, far from the issue being muted by a *"conspiracy of silence"*, [2] it had been openly discussed for at least seven years before it was overwhelmingly carried at the Yorkshire AGM in June 1893, and subsequently placed on the agenda at the Rugby Union's annual meeting.

As a preamble to Rugby Union's most historic national meeting, it is perhaps necessary, therefore, to air the full gamut of opinion on the subject, in the form of the brief anthology which concludes this chapter.

Apart from one notable exception, these viewpoints fall into one of a three categories. The majority of people appeared to see the broken-time proposal as simply a matter of *"amateurism versus professionalism"*, although, as *The Yorkshire Post* pointed out, *"Were it really a question of establishing acknowledged professionalism we do not think the proposal would have been carried by a majority of clubs in Yorkshire"*. [3] Others were also convinced that broken-time was a *"fraud"* when discussed in terms of *"pure amateurism"*, but they had come to the conclusion that full professionalism was therefore required. The middle ground, *"the moderate party"*, was taken by the advocates of broken-time who believed that such payments would not only eradicate the hypocrisy of *"veiled professionalism"* but would also establish *"a barrier"* against full professionalism, the latter which many commentators saw as threatening to bankrupt most Football League clubs. Only A. N. *"Monkey"* Hornby appears to have shown much originality of thought. He championed the broken-time proposal on the grounds that, if so-called amateurs in soccer and cricket could receive money for playing, then some payment ought not to be denied to working-class rugby players.

It was only the Lancashire President's surprising intervention, at a meeting held prior to the national AGM, which swung his county's vote in support of the Yorkshire resolution. The clubs themselves, of course, were later left to vote as they wished, and according to one report, *"Open professionalism would just as soon have been supported by messrs Clegg (Wigan), Warren (Warrington), Mills (Swinton) and Wilson (Rochdale Hornets) as was broken-time".*[4] Their views, however, were not representative of the county as a whole and only by 47 votes to 35 was it agreed to support Yorkshire's proposal.

Also added to the debate over the remuneration of players, and the *"dangers"* of imitating soccer, was the effect of leagues, and it is therefore necessary at this stage to describe the background to this movement. As we shall see in the anthology, northern opinion (*"Old Ebor"* and *"Nomad"*) was divided on the relationship between leagues and professionalism, whilst most southerners were said to have had *"an unreasonable horror of the term league",* equating it clearly with professionalism and the promotion of the game for gate-money rather than as an amateur pastime.[5]

This fear would not have been helped by the timing of the initial meeting at which proposals for a Yorkshire rugby league were first discussed. This was held in Wakefield on 3 May, 1889, the very same evening that the Football League held their first AGM.[6] It was argued that a high-pressure championship for twelve of the county's leading gate-taking clubs would be a truer test than the Yorkshire Cup in deciding which was the champion club. Furthermore, it would stimulate public interest throughout the season and increase gates, which, unlike the cup-ties, would be shared. Far from encouraging professionalism, its protagonists argued that the league's annual registration of players would provide *"a strict guard against professionalism".* The league proposal, however, received short shrift at most subsequent club AGMs, and Yorkshire later decided that any league must be under their authority.

Against the background of club suspensions and professional inquiries - as well as the fact that other minor competitions were already flourishing[7] - it was almost inevitable that the league scheme would be resurrected, and, sure enough, after the Oldham inquiry in 1890, one commentator suggested that, *"the formation of a league to acknowledge professionalism, to a certain extent, would be far better than..."veiled professionalism"* as at present.[8] Ever alive to such a daunting prospect,

Reverend Marshall successfully proposed at the Rugby Union's 1891 AGM that any league should be under its authority and power of veto. Nonetheless, by passing this resolution the Union effectively sanctioned the principal of leagues.

During March, 1892 an *Alliance* of ten of Yorkshire's major gate-taking clubs - Bradford, Batley, Dewsbury, Halifax, Huddersfield, Hunslet, Leeds, Liversedge, Wakefield Trinity and Brighouse Rangers - began to meet in private, and agreed to cancel fixtures with any club (as they later did with Leeds), which might decide to desert the cause of a self-governing league. In June, delegates from nine of the most influential clubs in Lancashire - Broughton Rangers, Oldham, St. Helens Recreation, Salford, Swinton, Warrington, Wigan, Liverpool, and Liverpool Old Boys (the latter two, together with Manchester, later declined to join) - also met to discuss a similar scheme, which they recommended to their county committee for approval. The Yorkshire clubs, on the other hand, continued to ignore their county executive.

Their clandestine activities, however, had not gone unnoticed, and, at a *"stormy"* Yorkshire AGM later that same month, Frank Marshall's resolution (seconded by the new President, James Miller), which required any proposed league to submit its rules to Yorkshire's annual meeting, was approved. The *Alliance* were also thwarted when they tried to bypass their own Union, as, predictably, the Rugby Union Committee, on 19 July, 1892, refused to sanction the proposal *"to form an alliance in Yorkshire and a league in Lancashire."*[9]

In order to help avoid a split in the Union the *Alliance*, whose membership had now changed with the withdrawal of Leeds and the inclusion of Manningham, agreed to a conference, on 8 August, at the conclusion of which they set out their main requirements, namely, the sanctioning of a self-managing *Yorkshire Senior Competition*, and the postponing of the Yorkshire Cup draw until the dispute had been resolved. However, because of the Rugby Union's earlier resolution, the Yorkshire committee, on 12 August, refused to meet either of these demands. Instead they proposed to submit a league scheme to the Rugby Union which would have included every Yorkshire club. As a consequence, on the following evening the ten *Alliance* clubs resigned their membership of Yorkshire Rugby Union and abandoned their scheme. Hull, who were later to become the eleventh senior club, also handed in their resignation.

After a Yorkshire special general meeting refused to accept the former *Alliance* clubs' resignations and agreed to delay the Cup draw, the crisis was finally resolved at a conference during August when James Miller submitted a scheme, which conceded the main points over self-management and league membership, but reserved the right of the county committee to override any decisions of this powerful sub-committee.[10] Both parties had therefore agreed on a settlement which would satisfy the Rugby Union, but it was an arrangement which was fraught with problems.

The history of the league movement in Yorkshire, and the danger of future revolt, was summed up by *"Old Ebor"* as follows:

*The insistence of the Yorkshire clubs on a competition managed by themselves, under authority, for themselves, is more than anything else an assertion of independence. The spirit which prompted it has been growing for years. There has been too marked a tendency on the part of the Yorkshire Union to increase its individual and collective power at the expense of the senior organisations by relying on the voting strength as distinct from the football influence of the young clubs of the county. The development of junior talent is one thing, but the levelling of clubs is another; and clubs which have spent thousands of pounds and years of labour building up the reputation of themselves and their county cannot be expected to remain at the mercy of every tin-pot organisation with a guinea, a ball, and a pair of goal posts, without a very energetic protest....*

*The resignation of the chief clubs caused the Yorkshire Unionists to effect a wonderfully rapid change in their view of the situation. All the more credit to them for it! They have found, and will find, that taking the chief clubs of Yorkshire by the hand affords a much easier method of locomotion than hooking them by the nose.*[11]

As we shall see, according to the above writer, the first league season in Yorkshire was marked by a unanimity of purpose between the county and the senior clubs, and this also appears to have been the case on the other side of the Pennines.

Although agitation for a league structure in Lancashire had also emanated from the senior gate-taking clubs, the issue had been handled in a rather more amicable fashion, only Manchester and Liverpool showing any opposition to the scheme which John Payne submitted to the Lancashire AGM in September, 1892. As well as a championship play-off, unlike Yorkshire, it embraced all the clubs in membership with the county, whilst promotion and relegation was agreed to from the outset. These were to be decided by means of *"test matches"* between the bottom and top clubs of each ten-club division.[12]

This scheme appears to have worked well in the first few seasons, but, as with the Yorkshire Senior Competition, the Lancashire First Class clubs were determined to protect their elitist position. As we shall see in the next volume, it was the conflict between these leading clubs and their respective counties, principally over the issue of promotion and relegation, which would directly bring about the split in rugby in 1895.

For the moment, however, we must return to the crucial debate over amateurism and professionalism, which dominated the early 1890s.

### Extracts from Professional Football: *A Plea for Legitimate Concessions* by "A Pro. in Mufti" in *The Yorkshireman Football Number*, March, 1891

Professionalism exists no longer! That is what we have been repeatedly told of late in Yorkshire. We have seen the same high-falutin stand-point of morality set up before us, only to find it ignominiously demolished by incontrovertible facts.....(Yorkshiremen) know that there is as much sub rosa professionalism in their own county to-day as ever....

But legalised professionalism in rugby circles is not wanted and is not necessary. Our rulers need to ask themselves the question: Is it advisable to continue making a show of heaven-born purity, or to manfully acknowledge our hypocrisy, and if not legalise professionalism outright, which I do not advocate - at any rate grant such legitimate concessions as the personal considerations which football men call for?

It is useless disguising the fact that football is no longer an academic sport, designed for aristocratic scions and eye-glassed collegians. It is a public institution and its exponents are public men. Those who indulge in the pastime play not only for their own recreation, enjoyment, and fame, but for the amusement of the public also. That is a feature which has hitherto escaped the consideration of the powers in high places, who in their anxiety to maintain a Quixotic standard of unadulterated amateurism, have forgotten that the exigencies of to-day and the circumstances of a decade back are very different articles. In the north the game is essentially dependent upon working men, both for its exposition and its support. It is a game by the masses for the masses... And the necessities of their public engagements make it incumbent upon players to sacrifice a considerable portion of their wage-earning time and labour in a cause which is as much that of the public as their own.

Is it fair that the players should alone bear the brunt of the pecuniary loss which the pursuit of the pastime necessarily involves? I know the quick retort will come "pat" from the lips of any-price amateurs, that football is a sport, not an occupation, and the man who cannot afford it to play for sport should let it alone. But to carry out such an abstract idea to its logical conclusion would be to depopularise the game, and make it a selfish possession of the silver-spooned classes.

Moreover, it would deprive the pastime of its ablest and most numerous exponents, who are essentially the working men of the north, and its most enthusiastic supporters, who are, undoubtedly the wage-earning classes. It follows, therefore, that the players who are called upon to sacrifice so much time and labour for the good of football should be entitled to fairer consideration than they can now obtain....

Refunding of actual monetary loss - no more, no less - is required. I commend this payment for broken-time doctrine to our Yorkshire Union, and to the rugby authorities at large. The granting of this concession to the legitimate demands of the working men footballers would be of far more service in resisting the advance of legalised professionalism than the present martinet policy, which regards the personal payment of shillings as a heinous crime, but which is powerless to prevent the disbursement of pounds by back-handed shufflings, on which the light is seldom shed.

### James Miller's address to the annual meeting of Yorkshire club secretaries, 10 April, 1891[13]

As you are all aware, there are at present very grave rumours that professionalism is in our midst, and I trust you will all fight against it as firmly as you have done in the past. The reason to do so is because professionalism would bankrupt the majority of our clubs, and would reduce the game almost to the level of arrow-throwing and rabbit coursing. Above all, professionalism ought to be resisted because it would ruin the game as a sport. That is a state of things very pitiful to contemplate, and yet you must all feel that we are drifting very rapidly towards it. I am convinced that unless something is done, and done quickly, professionalism will be a reality in a few years time.

In order to prevent such a state of affairs being brought about I should like to suggest three remedies. The first measure should be to limit the transfers and migration of players; to grant players reasonable concessions by allowing men to be paid loss of wages when breaking-time; and lastly to increase rather than diminish the penalties imposed for professionalism.

If these three measures were applied the ground would be cut from under the feet of such players, who had not only advocated professionalism but were working to bring it about. There is no doubt that the migration of players lays at the root of professionalism. It is hard to imagine the enthusiasm of a man leaving his work and travelling ten or fifteen miles for nothing to play a game no better than such as he could play on his own door, or in his own district. That anyone does such a thing without some inducement is difficult to believe, and therefore measures ought to be taken to prevent migration without sufficient reason.

Nonetheless, it was unreasonable to expect the same *"amateurism"* from the wage-earning classes as from public school men. It was unfair to expect working men to break time to play football without their being remunerated. What ought to be done was to take steps to legalise what was just in the matter, and so put an end to much veiled professionalism.

Nor was the Yorkshire Union itself perhaps free from reproach in the way of agreeing to the fixing of matches at times and on days when working men could not attend without loss of time....It would be far better if an equivalent for loss of time could be given openly and properly, and to adopt a system on similar basis to that which is worked for insurance at present. Returns of payments made might be sent in as was the case with insurance and should such returns be incorrect the punishment ought to be increased.

### Extracts from *Payment for Broken-time at Rugby Football* by Reverend F. Marshall in the *Athletic News Annual 1891/2*

How is it possible for a working man with a wage of from 15 to 25 shillings a week, perhaps with a wife and children to support, to play football unless he is compensated for loss of time? It is manifestly clear that the wage lost on Saturday morning is an appreciable factor in the provision for the week's expenses, and that the man can ill afford to lose the amount, though small it may be in actual cash. There can be no getting over this argument. It is clear and irrefutable.

The best point put forward is that, now that the clubs pay rail fares, provide teas, furnish the players with jerseys and boots, in fact, pay every legitimate expense - such payment for broken-time may well come within the expenses incurred by the player. Besides, players who may be in receipt of salaries paid quarterly, or of weekly wages independently of the hours worked, are manifestly on more advantageous terms than the player who is only paid for the time that he works. This again is an argument which cannot be gainsaid. But when the supporters of the principle go further, and say that it will not be the thin end of the wedge, that it will retard rather than advance the introduction of professionalism, there I beg leave to join issue with them....

In fact, the principle of payment for broken-time clearly establishes the principle of payment for playing football, and the principle once established will soon be carried out to its logical issue....payment for broken-time is the first step and the most direct step to professionalism.

It has been suggested that the system could be regulated and controlled as to render abuse impossible. Rubbish! If the Rugby Union cannot control and expose the secret payments that are undoubtedly made, how can they be expected to efficiently supervise payments which, under the guise of remuneration for broken-time, may easily be in reality payment for playing football? It is further argued that it is better for clubs to pay for this broken-time openly than in the secret way in which it is being done....Therefore why not allow an open payment and thus render the practice of this underhand remuneration unnecessary? But would the practice cease? Would not Oliver ask for more? Would not the underhand practice still go on, plus the payment for broken-time? Most probably....

But, in reply, let us consider how payment would affect the clubs and the game....The junior clubs have small gates; they have difficulty in even paying the railway fares of their players. The large clubs can offer attractions, such as all expenses paid, players insured at high rates; teas, dinners, and entertainments, and a holiday in the shape of a tour. If to these be added payment for broken-time, how are we to keep our players is the cry of the junior clubs? At present their good men leave them to join the first team of the premier club, and decline to become members of the second team. This is well known, and the second team of a large club is often very inferior to the first teams of its junior neighbours. But a large club having the money to pay its players for broken-time would command the services of any good player in the neighbourhood, who would wisely prefer to join the second team and get his wages unbroken at the week's end rather than stay with a club that could do nothing for him....

Lastly to the game. What effect would the system have upon the game and its players? I look upon the game....in two lights, viz, as an exhibition and as a sport. Now these two ideas are so diametrically opposed that we may take it that the struggle lies between these two views. Why is there the demand for the working man to leave his work and play football? Simply because the club wishes to win its matches, obtain a good record, give a good exhibition, please its spectators, and thus obtain a good gate and ample funds to carry on the club. This is the main idea predominating the lines on which most clubs carry on the campaign. Therefore the player must turn out at all costs. Without him the club record will suffer, and so all pressure and every inducement is brought to bear upon him in order to secure his services.

On the other hand, the game regarded as a sport is viewed in an entirely different light....It is emphatically a Saturday afternoon game; it is a game of little expense to the player, and therefore within the means of the working man both as to time and money, consequently no absolute necessity for the sacrifice of either work or money....I can read in the account of an English-Scotch match that Charlie Gurdon, then one of the three best forwards in England, was unable to play because he was on circuit. He did not neglect his profession for football....And this is but one instance in many.

I write with the conviction in my mind that professionalism will very probably come....As long as I take any interest in football, and as long as I have any influence in the game, my voice will be raised against any step that may imperil the Rugby Union as an amateur body, regarding the game as a sport, and to be conducted on that basis, and that alone.

It is far preferable to have two bodies, one amateur and the other professional, than to have the methods of the Association game imitated by the Rugby Union....Do not let us plead for the working man on a false issue. Let us advocate open professionalism, and if the British public calls for the article and will pay the piper, let us have paid players, properly remunerated, to satisfy the public taste. But in that case let them be outside the Rugby Union and a body of themselves.

### Extracts from *The Future of Rugby Football: Professionalism and the League* by *"Nomad"* in *The Yorkshireman Football Number*, March, 1892

That something is going to happen, bearing upon the conduct of the game in Yorkshire, everybody is agreed. What that something will consist of, and the probable date of its approach, are matters of pure speculation; but the interest fact remains that a change is impending....The very mention of the world *"professionalism"* used to excite pious horror in people's minds, and the subject was discussed with bated breath, where now it forms a regular topic of debate. This goes to prove that the once dreaded innovation is at least within the region of practical politics.

This question of payments is not one that can be quietly disposed of in Committee either at the Leeds or London centres. It is for the clubs to decide how they will go on, and I have very little doubt in my mind that they will some day take the law into their own hands and launch the ship of professionalism. The immediate result of such a course would naturally be excommunication, at the instance of the county executive (obeying the behest of the Rugby Union) but with a fair number of clubs in the plot no particular inconvenience would be experienced.

The public, who don't care a brass farthing about the social status of the players, would still patronise the strongest team, as they do now....Can anyone doubt that the strength would rest with the clubs who were employing paid talent? The comparison with the Association game is instructive enough on that point, and I know no reason why the argument should not apply to rugby with equal force....

We are now going through the same experiences in regard to rugby which formerly menaced the Association game - the veiled professionalism, the transfer difficulty, and the despotic government. These are what make the sport unendurable to the *bona fide* amateur, and the only cure is the legalisation of paid talent. If the rugby game could fairly be carried on in Yorkshire without this step being taken, the question would never be raised. It is not a party movement, for those who would profit by its adoption dare not utter one word in its favour. Cause and effect are forcing the matter into prominence, and it cannot be scotched by pure sentiment, as some writers appear to imagine.

How will the innovation really affect the play of our clubs? Football skill cannot be maintained except at a great sacrifice of time, trouble, and expense. There must be training, and no indulgence in excesses, otherwise the would-be player of today is soon shunted in favour of others, who have the time to attend to their condition.

Now, if these men are not fit subjects for remuneration, then all I can say is this: that the thousands who flock to witness their performances ought not to be charged an admission fee. *"But the gate money"*, argues the sentimentalist, *"often goes to charitable objects"*. Just so, only the worst of it is that charity is about the last thing in the average spectator's mind. He attends matches out of a love of the game, and those who provide the play ought, if they require it, by every human law (except those framed by the Rugby Union), to receive a share of the spectators' contributions. If it were so the players would naturally return the compliment by giving as good a display as possible....

Now about the evils which it is alleged payment of players will bring in its train. How about rough play and winning at any price! As to the first of these items, it seems to me that with the same stringent regulations in force as at present there would be a minimum of rough play, for the simple reason that suspension to the professional would mean a matter of life and death. Style must, in my opinion, also greatly improve, because, when all is said and done, few matches are won by mere force, and with men making a thorough study of the game they would be sure to develop its scientific methods in the end. One thing is quite certain, viz., that the rough-and-tumble scrambles seen in the Cup-ties could hardly be perpetrated by paid *"artistes"*.

Betting, they say, would be rife under the new regime - as if it could be any rifer than it is today! In spite of all the gush and boasting about the existing purity of football, it is a fact that never a match is played without some betting being done. I have heard persons coolly assert that one or the other match has been sold, but I do not believe that an actually instance of such a thing has ever happened. It would be impossible to do it without the fraud coming to light, and the idea would occur last of all to the man whose services were being properly remunerated.

The veiled professional might be guilty of such conduct or the impecunious amateur, but not the wage-earner. It is childish to connect betting with professionalism in that way, and yet I have seen such theories in print, coupled with an expression of thankfulness that Rugby Unionists are not as other men (Associationists). Well, as for that, I noticed the other day that 25,000 spectators assembled at Sheffield to see a Cup-tie between Sunderland and Aston Villa - two out-and-out professional teams. What a reflection on the alleged *"waning of interest"* and *"hopeless state of affairs"*, which the dribbling game is said to have developed!....

The league scheme is expected to reach maturity very shortly by its chief adherents, but I must say that in my opinion it cannot be properly worked in Yorkshire under the present government. It is feared as too big a rival to the county programme to inspire the Union with any sympathy for it. Of course, certain clubs might reply, *"We will have our league in spite of you"*, and if they go so far as that they may just as well adopt professionalism, for their sentence will be the same in either case. It seems to me that the two are inseparably bound up together, for a league in Yorkshire means additional organisation and more reserve strength to draw upon in time of need.

At present there is no reserve worth mentioning attached to any of our crack clubs. The first team is sorted out and the remainder immediately betakes itself to fresh fields where talent is scarce. Payment alone will induce these reserves to stick to their colours. Other sources of reply have been ruthlessly cut off by the Union which has made it almost impossible for a good club to enrol promising playing members during the season. The irritation caused by this means has undoubtedly shaken the foundations upon which the government is constructed. This it is, among other grievances, which has given a fillip to the league project as a possible relief from official oppression.

I have said that I think a league would result in professionalism. I am still more certain that payment would induce the formation of a league because it would be necessary to provide extra attractions in order to cope with enormously increased expenses. The order of the day with our clubs has been viz., occasional excitement for special fixtures, with a possibility of a haul out of Cup-ties. The league would sustain the interest throughout, besides being a far safer medium of profit than any other kind of enterprise - only, clubs would be able to rely upon a set of strong players to make the affair a success. With men called away on county or international duty incessantly your league team could not go the pace without a few good reserves....

In conclusion, I would point out that this article is merely intended to show the impossible nature of the existing condition of football in

Yorkshire. I regard professionalism as a necessary evil, but the lesser evil of two which are staring us in the face. Either we must have professionalism with law and order or compulsory amateurism with increased irregularities, oppression and disorder. Needless to add which alternative will find acceptance in the end. My advice to clubs is to economise and save up all they can, to drop extravagant feasting and touring, and put something by for *"Wages Account"*.

### Extracts from *Past Development in Rugby Football and The Future of the Game* by Arthur Budd in Reverend F. Marshall *Football: The Rugby Union Game*, published in 1892

To begin with, if one were asked to define *"sport"*, it ought to be described as a recreation pursued for love of itself, and devoid of emolument....whatever branch of athletics an entrance has been opened for profit without amateur supervision, at the same door hand in hand there has stepped in also the element of corruptibility. Secondly, is it not an incontrovertible axiom that a man who gives his whole time and energies to a game is bound to outstrip another who only devotes his leisure moments to its pursuit?....The answer, then, to those who urge that the working man ought to be compensated for the *"loss of time"* incurred by his recreation is that, if he cannot afford the leisure to play a game, he must do without it.

How many splendid athletes are never heard of again when they leave their universities and schools, because they have to follow avocations which will not allow them to play football matches, which necessitate one, two, or three days desertion of their profession?

If A.B. of the Stock Exchange were to ask for compensation for loss of time for a two-days' football tour, such compensation to be fixed on a scale commensurate with his earnings, the football community would denounce it as a scandal. A. B., the stockbroker, has therefore to stop at his desk because he cannot afford to play, but C. D., the working man, is to be allowed his outing and compensation for leaving his work, which under any other circumstances he could not afford to abandon....

If ever a vivid illustration of the gradual process of amateur extinction were afforded to us, the Rugby Unionists, as though by Providence, it has been the history of the Association game from the day that this body legitimised professionalism. I am correct, I believe, in saying that in the whole of the north of England and the Midlands, there is not a single amateur football eleven. What does this mean? Why, that amateurs in those districts have been submerged by professionals, and have to seek other modes of recreation than Association football for their leisure. But a few years ago such clubs as Old Carthusians were competitors in the final tie of the Association Cup; this year every southern amateur team was beaten in the first round of the ties....

Does (professionalism) encourage native or recreational talent, which, mark you, should be the first and only object of every football club? On the contrary, it leads to the wholesale importation of players of repute from other districts or, it may be, countries, to the exclusion of the indigenous ability. Is this sport? I say, certainly not. It is nothing more nor less than handing over success in the game to the best capitalised club. If you could give me the wealth of the Duke of Westminster and professionalism in Rugby football to boot, I would in a very short time produce the most formidable fifteen in the United Kingdom.....

If....blind enthusiasts of working men's clubs insist on introducing professionalism, there can be but one result - disunion. The amateur must refuse to submit himself to the process of slow extinction which has been going in the sister game, and say at once, that henceforth he will play and compete with own class alone, and let professionals for the future look amongst themselves for opponents.

And if this black day comes, which I hope it never will, it will be the duty of the Rugby Union to see that the division of classes dates from the dawn of professionalism, and not to wait, before seeking to apply a remedy as the short-sighted Associationists have done, to see the whole of the north and part of the south denuded of amateurs and given up to subsidised players. To them the charge of a game of great traditions has been committed, and, if they would be willing to consign the future of these to the baneful influence of professionalism, they would assuredly be betraying the trust reposed in them, and live regretfully to see the game of today depraved, degraded, and decayed.

### Competition Football in Yorkshire - Has it Proved a Success? by "Old Ebor" in The Yorkshireman Football Number, March, 1893

One marked feature about competition football is the change in the attitude which the Yorkshire rulers have adopted towards it. Not more than nine months ago Mr Miller condemned the league movement as being promoted by clubs "on the downward grade" for sinister purposes. The clubs on the downward grade finish in the first four, one of them holds the Shield, another held the Yorkshire Cup, and a third plays perhaps the best football in the county. But on the 21st inst., speaking as the President of the Yorkshire Union, Mr Miller said the winners of the Shield "stood out by the fairest method of trial"...I rather take the pleasure of believing that the latest remarks show that the Yorkshire President has misunderstood the competition system in its inception, and the frank and handsome manner in which the system is now approved suggests that he is not ashamed to recognize the mistakes of earlier times....

One charge made against the league system in its incubating days was that it was meant to increase gates and encourage professionalism. It has not done the latter and has only partially resulted in the former. The increasing of gates is inevitably associated with the repute of a team....Of course, this is no new feature; it was shown in club football before the competitionists appeared on the scene. Striking the general average, the patronage accorded to competition games has been certainly ahead of that seen at ordinary club engagements, and the clubs who have done best in football have been favoured the most in patronage, a fact to be demonstrated in the statement that in their nine home competition games the Bradford club has taken £1,500.

Another charge brought against the competitionists was that by their policy they would increase roughness and depreciate the general style of play. The very opposite has proved the fact....I think I am correct in saying that only two, or three at the outside, have been reported during the season for roughness in a competition game, and even they were charged with comparatively trivial offences....

The payment of players is certainly a season nearer accomplishment but that is because of the march of time and not in consequence of the competition movement. The rugby authorities are treating the professional question pretty much as a timid child regards the bogey-man of nursery lore. We are asked to keep out the pest at any price and to take warning by the *"shocking example"* of the Associationists - the example of one of the finest, best played, and most popular sports in the world! Professionalism will come, must come; and when it does arrive rugby clubs will benefit by the mistakes and the experience of their Association forerunners.

But the time has not yet come, and a means to postpone it - not to obviate it, for that is impossible - is to grant payment for *bona fide* broken-time, regarding which I am glad to notice that Mr Miller is again going to sound public opinion through the medium of the Yorkshire Union. Payment for broken-time would assist the competition movement immensely; and here I may remark that the past season has been remarkable for the extent to which football-men have exercised self-sacrifice by breaking time in the interest of the competition matches. The exigencies of modern football, however, demand in an ordinary season a considerable degree of broken-time, and payment for this will be conceded if Yorkshire speaks with no uncertain voice. To my mind the argument which permits the refunding of out-of-pocket expenses and refuses payment of money, kept from entering the pocket, is absurd and illogical....what can be a greater expense to the working man than the loss of a half-day's wage?....The season's working has proved that there is room for competition football, county loyalty, and cup-tie success, and that the interests of all are practically identical.

### *Professionalism in Football by O.P.Q.* in *The Yorkshireman*, **September, 1893**

It is fortunate for the patrons of the rugby game that they have the opportunity of judging of the evil results of the payment system in another branch of football....Without doubt, professionalism has proved ruinous to Association clubs. About the only Association organisation in a sound, solvent position today is Everton, and just consider their items of expenditure for last season. Their gate receipts came to £9,915, and of that amount they have to expend in players' wages alone the sum of £3,529. But this position of affairs is very exceptional, even in Association circles. Sunderland were at the head of the Association League at the end of last season, and I understand that a £10 note will cover their balance for 1892/3. Preston North End came second, but consider how they stand financially. It is estimated that at the present time the club is insolvent to the extent of £1,400. Aston Villa followed Everton on the League list, and, although their income was £5,208, their working expenses exceeded that amount by £273....I ask, after reading those figures, what reasonable man can recommend the adoption of professionalism in rugby circles? For, let it be remembered, that whilst we play fifteen men, they put in the field only eleven....

Even Bradford could not afford to pay their men, and that club is the most successful financially in connection with the rugby game. At the end of last season they had a balance to the good of about £1,164; but supposing they had to pay their men how far would that go? It is plain to see that once professionalism were adopted the balance of even the Bradford club would be as much on the wrong side as it is now on the good. But what would become of the other prominent organisations? There is Dewsbury with a deficit of £200, Brighouse has a balance due to the treasurer of £9, Halifax are on the wrong side of the balance sheet, Hunslet has a favourable balance of £388, and Manningham has £310 in the bank. Leeds, however, are well on the wrong side, whilst Wakefield can show only a balance of £77. And mark you, all this apart from any expense in the form of payment of players.

I need not go into the balance sheets of some of the minor clubs, for their position is, of course, such that they could not, for a moment, entertain the idea of professionalism. *"But"*, it has been said, *"you could limit the pay."* Could you? It is prohibited today and yet it exists; how then, when open dealing is allowed, are you going to prevent competition, and with it the certain advance in the salaries the men are able to command?

That some reform is necessary, I admit, but the experience of the Association clubs warns us from the payment of players as professionals, unless we are anxious to run headlong into bankruptcy. The solution of the difficulty is to be found in the payment for broken-time, and a maximum rate per day should be fixed for that. But whatever is the outcome of the discussion (on the 20 September, 1893), of this I am certain, professionalism will mean ruin to rugby football clubs.

### From *The Bradford Observer*, 18 September, 1893.

There is a slight suspicion that some of the most ardent advocates of Mr Miller's scheme are actuated solely by motives of self defence or economy. The expenses of the big clubs have lately grown to a frightful extent and perhaps a peep behind the scenes would convince the sceptical that amateur sport may become even more costly than its disparaged rival. Professionalism is worked on recognised lines. Amateurism simply pretends to be and what the difference amounts to in money today no man can tell. Unless a decided check is put upon the lavish expenditure of clubs a general state of bankruptcy must ensue before long. There will be at least a fixed scale of payment, limiting the liability, whereas some of today's amateurs appear to involve their clubs in costs which can never be properly estimated beforehand. In this way we can perhaps understand how the Yorkshire proposal comes to be designated as a *"safeguard"* against professionalism. Viewed from the point of safeguarding pure amateur sport, however, Mr Miller's proposal looks rather like a fraud....Linked with the latter (amateurism) it does not deserve to succeed, and we know that the Rugby Union will move heaven and earth to get it defeated on Wednesday evening next.

How the voting will turn out depends almost entirely upon what the Union have up their sleeves in the way of new members. Speaking from experience, we should say that they must be pretty strong, or they would hardly try to get rid of Yorkshire's proposal by moving the direct negative. The English Rugby Union have always excelled in diplomacy, and they generally temporise with unavoidable troubles, only putting their foot down when confident of carrying their point.

# Chapter Eight
# The Broken-Time Meeting
## *"A Triumph for Veiled Professionalism"*

The venue for the most important general meeting in the Rugby Union's history was the mammoth 286-room Westminster Palace Hotel, which was situated at the east end of Victoria Street, near to Westminster Abbey. At its opening in 1860 it was the most luxurious hotel in London, with its principal function being to provide accommodation for members of Parliament and visitors to the Law Courts. On the evening of 20 September, 1893, however, the entrance was alive to nothing but talk of rugby legislation and rugby politics, as hundreds of delegates headed for the hotel's spacious coffee room.[1] It was later suggested that some of the Yorkshire representatives - who early that morning had arrived at King's Cross aboard a special twelve-carriage excursion - did not attend this crucial meeting, having *"lost their way in the great Metropolis as countrymen are occasionally supposed to do".*[2] It is highly likely that this comment from George F. Berney, who at the time of the meeting was a member of the Rugby Union committee and President of Surrey, was meant as a slur on the intelligence of northerners generally, but it may also have contained an element of truth in so far as the Westminster Palace Hotel was *"courageously situated some distance away from any of the main railway termini".*[3]

Even without these possible northern absentees, it was still the largest gathering in the Rugby Union's 22-year history, whilst the atmosphere within the crowded meeting room was also said to have been unprecedented. *"The opening,"* Berney recalled, *"was preceded by the strange and uncanny silence which often heralds the settlement of great issues by the ordeal of battle."* Thereafter it was the unenviable task of the President, William Cail of Northumberland,[4] to maintain order of a what turned out to be an uproarious meeting. This was not only due to the emotive subject, but principally because of the ill-feeling which flowed from the large Yorkshire contingent towards Reverend Marshall. Unfortunately, whilst it has been possible to quote some speeches almost verbatim, the general behaviour of the delegates can only be left to the reader's imagination.[5]

After the formal business had been rapidly dispensed with, the President called upon James Miller to move the Yorkshire resolution, *"That players be allowed compensation for bona fide loss of time"*, but W. P. Carpmael (Blackheath) immediately rose to question whether the rules on professionalism permitted such a resolution. William Cail then explained that, as it would entail a change in the bye-laws, the resolution needed a two-thirds majority to be carried, and the committee would then be morally bound to submit well-defined rules to a further general meeting for approval. *"Using temperate language and in a quiet self-possessed manner"*, James Miller was then allowed to proceed:

*I am fully aware of the gravity of the question and I hope that this meeting will consider it impartially. Why have we brought this proposal forward? Simply because of the changed conditions under which rugby football is now played. That change, I believe, has been brought about by the action of this Union in fostering the game. Formerly it was only played by the public schools, the Universities, and the favoured classes, but the game has now become the great winter pastime of the young working men of this country. This is particularly the case in the great manufacturing centres of the north of England. The Union, unfortunately, still declines to recognize this new type of player. We recognize him in the north and we treat him differently to what we would have done some years ago.*

*The question is one which this night will be decided by the votes of the southern representatives. (Cries of "no, no") and I hope you will endeavour to realise the difficulties, which we in the north have to deal with and which people in the south know nothing about (loud cries of "no, no" and the President called the meeting to order). The working man has to leave his work and lose his wages to play for the benefit of his club, his county or his country, but he received no recompense for the loss of wages. Was that fair, right or reasonable? These men naturally ask why they should have to play on such disadvantageous terms compared to the solicitor, the stockbroker, the clerk or the undergraduate. Why should they take part in matches at a loss to themselves?*

*Take the case of the England v. Ireland match which was played last year in Dublin, in which gentlemen players and working men players took part. They had to leave home on Friday morning, play on the Saturday, and Monday was the most favourable day for them to return home. The working men had their railway fare and hotel bills paid but found themselves at the end of the week minus three days wages, while the gentlemen players who took part in the match lost nothing. Do you call that playing on level terms?*

*I have no desire to make football a source of profit to the player, but equally it was not meant that players should play it at such a loss. If it was legitimate to refund expenses, why not refund lost wages? We wish to remove an injustice, and*

140

*we have the true interests of the game at heart as much as anyone in this room. Please don't pooh-pooh it simply because it comes from a county which is not always a savoury morsel to others.* (Laughter). *In concluding I believe that if the proposal was carried it would raise the strongest barrier against professionalism that has yet been devised.* (Applause).

After the proposal was seconded by Mark Newsome (Yorkshire), William Cail, without rising from his chair, proposed that:

*"This meeting, believing that the principle of the Yorkshire resolution is contrary to the true interests of the game and its spirit, declines to sanction the same."* As this was simply a negative proposal he later withdrew it and took the vote on the original resolution. The President then continued:

*I compliment Mr Miller on his moderation but think that he has somewhat overstepped the mark in appearing to speak as though he represented the whole of the north. I can speak for four more northern counties than Yorkshire, and I can say that there are not more than one or two clubs in these counties which are going to support his motion.*

*Mr Miller argued that the working man lost many hours wages, but I contend that the clerk who plays football is the greater loser in the long run. If an employer has two clerks, one of whom is constantly asking for leave off to play football, and the other constantly has his nose at the grindstone, when it comes to a case of promotion, which of these men will get it?*

*With regard to the Irish match, I was there with three players from my own district. They had to travel much further than Mr Miller's friends, yet they were back to business on Monday morning. Those who didn't get back could have been in no great hurry!*

*I should like to ask any players who are present whether they would wish to be bought and sold like association professionals? I am inclined to agree with the majority of the press - who are generally good judges - when they say that payment for broken-time is tantamount to the introduction of professionalism. This is objectionable, I believe, to a large majority of the clubs, many of whom will be unable to pay their members even if they are at liberty to do so. The result will be that whilst a few clubs with large gates will flourish others will be killed off.* (Loud cheers).

Continuous and loud cheering greeted Rowland Hill when he rose to second the amendment:

*I have never previously felt it necessary to advise on matters which were so divided but the time has now arrived when it is my duty to speak out. If the resolution is passed it must inevitably lead towards professionalism. What this resolution means is paying men for playing football.* (Loud applause). *What would be the effect on the working man? The temptation to play rugby was too great already. The opportunities were so many that a man might be away a whole week, and thus earn his wages without doing a single stroke of work. Mr Miller* has not given one practical suggestion as to how his scheme would be carried out. If carried it must break up the Union, and much as I should regret this it would be preferable to have division than professionalism. (Loud cheers).

The Rugby Union secretary was then followed by the monocled J. W. H. Thorp, the President of Cheshire[(6)]:

*I oppose the resolution on the grounds that it is against the true interests of British sport and rugby football. I wish to see the game played as it was twenty to twenty-five years ago and the amateur game kept pure for our children. Working men were genuine sportsmen and if we passed this resolution we will degrade them to a very much lower level. The pseudo working man and bastard amateur do not represent the working man of this country.* (Cheers and groans). *The latter, and I don't mean the working man who gets a transfer from one club to another which places him in a public-house, do not want this miserable subterfuge of broken-time payment* (Applause).

H. E. Steed (Surrey) then attempted to read out some statistics, which he said represented the opinions of northern clubs on the issue, but, stated *Pastime*, *"as his remarks brought forth a storm of disapproval from the Yorkshire contingent and did not appear to please the officials he abruptly concluded"*.

Mark Newsome (Yorkshire) then gave his reasons for supporting the motion:

*Nobody has done more to suppress professionalism than the Yorkshire Rugby Union. We speak from the experience of having had to fight professionalism more than any other county in England. At present the working man was the only class of player who suffered anything by playing football. It is said that broken-time would ruin the smaller organisations, but transfers from the smaller to the larger organisations were already carried on wholesale. By empowering clubs to give compensation for broken-time we will deprive these players of the excuse which they now have for migrating.* (Applause).

Considerable excitement was then aroused when Reverend Marshall rose to address the meeting, and after a loan voice had asked, *"What club?"*, his reply: *"Almondbury Grammar School"*, was greeted with both hilarity and applause. Frank Marshall then proceeded:

*It needs little ingenuity to show that this motion means professionalism. The Yorkshire Union might be described as a body which, instead of endeavouring to suppress professionalism, was really seeking to devise a means by which it could evade the laws. This motion is simply a "Relief Bill". Clubs in Yorkshire were getting enormous gates and wanted, naturally, to have the best players to maintain this support.*

*Many club secretaries tell me of the great strain to which they are put to meet this demand. In one club in Yorkshire there are seven publicans, while I am told that in the Yorkshire team last year there were eleven players either directly or*

142

*indirectly connected with public houses. It was absurd to suppose that the working man felt it a sacrifice to play for his county. If I were to advertise, inviting working men to have two or three days in London, travelling in saloons, having the best meals, and going to the theatres or music halls, all free of expense, thousands would willingly give up three days' wages for such a trip.* (At this stage the speaker alluded to the fact that, *"refreshments and cigars"* were *"among the more pleasant features of county matches"*, which was greeted with cries of *"bosh"* from the Yorkshire contingent).

*Even with the safeguard of a medical certificate behind it the Yorkshire Union has been unable to stop their insurance scheme from being abused, so how could they manage to regulate the proposed payments for broken-time? There is every indication that professionalism in the rugby game - I refuse to say the Rugby Union - must come; but I implore the meeting to vote straight on the question of professionalism, and not on a side issue. It is idle to say that this is a barrier against professionalism, when they all knew it was the first step towards its adoption.* (Applause).

Marshall's speech was greeted with cries of derision from most of the Yorkshire delegates, one of whom, J. H. Fallas, the Wakefield Trinity secretary,[7] was cautioned by the chair for describing Marshall as *"a political mountebank"*. When he continued in the same vein, William Cail refused to hear him and bellowed at him to, *"Sit down!"* Most Yorkshire speakers made some uncomplimentary remarks about the *"wearer of broadcloth"*, as one delegate called him, whilst Mr Tattersall of Bowling, Bradford, even suggested, amid roars of laughter, that it was because he could no longer avail himself of the free trips and cigars at Yorkshire's expense that Frank Marshall was now opposed to broken-time!

It was left to Harry Garnett (Otley), who later cautioned James Miller over his attitude towards Reverend Marshall, to restore some dignity to the proceedings. *"I am reluctantly compelled to support the resolution"*, said the former President of the Rugby Union, *"as I believe that professionalism is inevitable, and broken-time will at least postpone its advent for a few years. I would point out that, as regards the hardship of working men players, I know of one player who returned from Dublin the same night in order not to lose his wages. We should recognize the different conditions under which the game is now played.*

Garnett's Otley colleague and Yorkshire treasurer, J. Gledstone, in a clumsy speech which produced derisive laughter, believed that the main point had been missed:

*It was only bona fide payment for loss of time that would be allowed. Only when a player had bonafidely* (a term used by several other speakers) *lost his wages would he be refunded. The real question is: "Are you going to impose a penalty on the working man and not on the gentleman amateur?*

This gained a response from Reverend G. T. Warner (Devon) who claimed:

*We have a number of working men clubs in our county and yet none are in favour of broken-time. Indeed, in the west they not only give up their time but subscribe to the expenses of their clubs.*

F. C. Cousins (Oxford University and Richmond) then, "*mildly endeavoured to say a few words on behalf of the much-despised gentlemen amateurs*", whom, he said, often lost more than the working man:

*While Middlesex could never get its full team together when playing in Yorkshire, the northern team very rarely have any of its best working-class players absent. Rugby football was a game for amateurs, and professionals in disguise have no business with it. They entered the Union as amateurs and if they did not wish to continue as amateurs they should leave the Union.*

Thus far nothing had been heard from the Midlands but K. B. Holmes (Midland Counties) informed the meeting that:

*The 51 clubs in my district are almost entirely composed of working men and they are satisfied if they are allowed rail fares and reasonable hotel expenses. None of the clubs, I might add, are in favour of the resolution. If the motion is adopted I believe the smaller clubs will be forced out of existence by the richer clubs.*

An indication that there were a number of junior clubs in Yorkshire which agreed with this speaker, was given by Mr Northin, the Bowling Old Lane (Bradford) representative, who expressed a similar fear that the legalisation of broken-time would mean extinction for his club.

Seemingly, therefore, Yorkshire's ranks were not all that united, and the known division in Lancashire was made apparent from the next two speakers. The former Manchester international forward of the 1870s, Roger Walker, who was then a Rugby Union vice-president, repeated many of Reverend Marshall's earlier points:

*I don't think that any proper scheme could be formulated for defining where this broken-time should begin and end - there would probably need to be two or three financial men at each club. It would also create discontent among the players as one man would receive more than another. I have experienced this at my local cricket club where some players receive broken-time. One player, whose wages were small, practically won the match by his performance, while another, whose wages were higher, had done nothing towards the victory. The proposition means professionalism, and this would probably flourish in Lancashire and Yorkshire, and if these counties want it they should separate themselves from the Rugby Union.*

There were signs that this restless gathering had heard enough of the arguments, but, amid cries of "*vote*", the former Swinton player and present club secretary, Joe Mills, just had time to put the official Lancashire case:

*As the Lancashire delegate I support the resolution. I am quite sure that the 47-35 votes, by which my Union agreed to support the resolution, does not fully represent the feelings within the county as a whole, as the more the question is discussed the stronger is the feeling in favour. The working men, who chiefly compose the teams in Yorkshire and Lancashire, feel that instead of Unions and clubs wasting funds on tours and dinners, some of this money, which they have helped earn, would be better spent on themselves and their families.*

James Miller was then called upon to reply:

*I expected Mr(sic) Marshall to oppose the resolution. It is too delicious a piece of pie for him to miss having his finger in. I have seen him cartooned...*(the President then rose to stop the speaker after Harry Garnett had objected to his colleague's remarks).

Reverend Marshall: *Oh, Mr Chairman, let him go on, I don't care.*

James Miller: *I have seen Mr Marshall cartooned as an old washerwoman, trying to sweep back the tide of professionalism with a broom, and I feel he is only following out that calling by his actions tonight. I object, however, to Mr Marshall making himself out to be a lamb with a white fleece, as I know a story which, if told, would cause some very black spots on the fleece. Do you believe this motion is the thin end of the wedge of professionalism.* (Cries of *"Yes"* and *"No"*). *The thin edge of the wedge had entered into rugby football years ago and is so firmly embedded that this Union, or any Union, is powerless to remove it. Unfortunately, it has assumed the form of the "bastard amateur" mentioned by Mr Thorp, and I think it should be looked at in that way. It is here and the best thing is to try and direct the wedge in a proper way, so that it does not split the whole fabric. It is far better to introduce a scheme which could be revised and pay working men for broken-time, in order that things which are now done stealthily can be carried out in the light of day.*

When the resolution was then put to the meeting the show of hands was clearly against it, and William Cail declared, *"The noes have it"*. However, James Miller and Barron Kilner requested a ballot, and it was not until a few minutes after ten o'clock that the figures - 282 votes against broken-time and 136 in favour - were finally announced. If we add the eight scrutineers, who had been paired and did not vote, and five spoilt papers, we arrive at a total of 431, which, from the minutes of the meeting, were made up of 414 clubs and Unions, plus the 17-man committee. George Berney later wrote that, *"When the vote was taken and its result announced by the chairman there was a burst of applause that might have shaken the walls of the Abbey"*, and a report at the time stated that the rejoicing lasted fully five minutes. According to one northern newspaper, however, there was very little to celebrate, as, in its opinion, the decision not to grant the working man his lost wages was merely *"a triumph for veiled professionalism"*.[8]

Be that as it may, with the above attendance, James Miller's proposal would have needed the support of at least another 140 clubs in order to have achieved the necessary two-thirds majority - in other words, he needed to completely reverse the above result. It may seem, therefore, that after such a decisive ballot there would be little need for further comment or speculation.

However, 100 years after the meeting, there are a number of questions which still need to be answered. These relate to alleged malpractices by the southern Rugby Union establishment in manipulating the voting procedure, which most modern-day historians (including, unfortunately, this writer) have previously assumed have had some significant bearing on the final outcome. Emphasis in the past has been placed on the use of proxy votes, and votes from the various Oxford and Cambridge University colleges, the latter which, allegedly, were not entitled to vote. We therefore need to eliminate these two contentious issues.

Although prior to the meeting some Yorkshire newspapers were aware that the southerners were *"working up their own clientele"*, and the subject has been vaguely hinted at in the above account of the meeting, the evidence that proxy votes were used comes almost entirely from George Berney. This is what he said happened after Yorkshire gave notice of their proposal for broken-time in June, 1893:

*A private committee was immediately formed in London, with F. Innes Currey[9] as chairman (if my memory is to be trusted), in order to organise the amateur forces of Rugby Football against any such proposal. The meetings were usually held at the Sports Club, St. James's Square, and there a circular was eventually drafted over the names of about 70 prominent football men, containing an appeal from those clubs of the Rugby Union who were presumed to be in sympathy with its objects. The credit of what followed in the history of the movement entirely belongs to H. E. Steed (Lennox FC)....He provided for a full poll of all the clubs who were to oppose the motion, and he found proxies for 120 of these who for various reasons could not attend the meeting. So well had his plans been laid that, some days before, he was able to indicate almost correctly the total of the votes to be cast on each side.[10]*

Even though Berney's memory and judgement apparently failed him when he wrote in the same essay about other matters; namely, when he said that the Northern Union was formed at the Mitre Hotel, Leeds; and that, prior to the broken-time meeting, new clubs in Yorkshire were formed, *"not solely by reason of natural necessity, but to some extent for the purpose of adding weight at the General Meetings by means of the faggot vote"*; there is still every reason to believe him on the subject of the above proxies.

There can be little doubt that they existed, but what form did they actually take, and was the proxy system part of the Rugby Union's normal procedure at general meetings? On the first point, several newspaper reports refer to the fact that over 400 delegates attended the meeting, which clearly indicates that the 120 proxy voters (who did not affect the result) were required to attend in person. In order to clarify this, however, we need only to refer to the 1891 AGM, when Yorkshire's proposal, to hold general meetings alternately in the north and south, failed to gain the necessary two-thirds majority, partly through Lancashire opposition. Whilst arguing that such a move would have practically disenfranchised many clubs in the south and the south-west, which had no gate-money to defray their delegate's expenses, H. G. Fuller (Cambridge University) made the statement, *"A club that cannot send a delegate can usually find and old member resident in London to attend the meeting".*[11] Therefore, as well as emphasising the importance of London for the southerners' retention of power, this would also appear to effectively answer the query over the nature of such proxies.

This was also confirmed in 1894 when *The Yorkshireman* acquired a similar circular to the one referred to by Berney. This read: *"If your club is unable to send a representative to the meeting, please sign the ticket as soon as received, and forward to Mr H. E. Steed at the above address, who will find someone to represent your club."* Not surprisingly, no offer was made to find proxies for Yorkshire clubs, nor for clubs in opposition to southern opinion, and there is no doubt, of course, that this also applied in 1893. If they had, however, it is unlikely that this would have materially affected the Yorkshire representation at the broken-time meeting, as even the delegate from that county's self-confessed poorest club, Harrogate, managed to travel down to London on Yorkshire's chartered train.

There was no reported outcry from this large Yorkshire contingent, either over the use of proxies or whether the proxy voters themselves were genuine existing, or former, club members. Nonetheless, for a number of years there had been some concern that many of the junior clubs - for whom, of course, Steed's proxy service had been designed - had not paid their subscriptions to the Rugby Union. For example, at the 1891 AGM Mr Slater of Holbeck had failed to discover whether the number of representatives present that night actually coincided with the list of paid-up member clubs.[12] Such a crucial fact appears to have eluded all but the treasurer and secretary, chiefly due to the high turnover of clubs throughout the season.

What is known, however, is that, according to the accounts presented to the 1893 AGM, 430 clubs had paid their subscriptions[13] Throughout the summer this figure must have increased by 51, *("The membership is likely to have materially increased during the year and it is just possible that a goodly number of little clubs have been unearthed in the south since last season")* [14] as, at the time of the broken-time meeting, the number of clubs in membership worldwide was said to be 481. [15]

Given these numbers, therefore, what effect was the voting strength of the Universities to have on the rejection of broken-time? This is easily answered by the following analysis of the 414 clubs and unions which were represented at the Westminster Palace Hotel: overseas unions 8, London (Kent, Middlesex and Surrey) 80, Eastern Counties 30, Midland Counties 26, South West Counties 28, Oxford and Cambridge University (including colleges) 13 and 16 respectively, and Newport (Monmouthshire). [16] The northern counties were represented as follows: Yorkshire 142, Lancashire 25, Cumberland and Westmoreland 14, Durham 17, Northumberland 9, and Cheshire [17] 5. If we add the members of the Rugby Union committee to the above figures we find that, geographically, the representation was fairly evenly divided - namely, 212 clubs and unions north of the River Trent, plus 9 committee, as opposed to 202 clubs and unions plus 8 committee, south of that river.

It is obvious, therefore, that, whatever contemporary writers may have said - for example, *"Amateur"* [18] referred to *"northerners,"* being *"outvoted through the sudden introduction of votes from all the Oxford and Cambridge colleges"* - the votes of the University colleges, legitimite or otherwise, were insignificant. What was of far more importance was the lack of support given to the Yorkshire committee's proposal by the other northern counties, by working-class clubs in the Midlands and the south-west, and by much of their own junior membership.

In Lancashire, apart from the county's vote, support for broken-time certainly came from the following First Class Competition clubs: Oldham, Swinton, Warrington, Tyldesley, Salford, Broughton Rangers, Rochdale Hornets, and Barrow. Broughton were the only club in this league to have opposed broken-time, and, after a 45-3 defeat by Oldham, one journalist commented, *"Apparently the club is as much behind its compeers in football skill as it is on the question of policy and management."* [19] Rochdale St. Clements of the Second Class Competition are also known to have voted in favour, [20] and there may also have been a few others among the small Lancashire contingent, which was approximately two-thirds of that county's membership within the Rugby Union. Ironically, although Wigan proposed broken-time at the Lancashire meeting, they were the only first-class Lancashire club which failed to make an appearance at the Westminster Palace Hotel.

It is fairly obvious that William Cail gained his information, on the voting intentions of clubs in the four most northern counties, from Steed's meticulous enquiries. If we therefore accept that only two or three clubs in those counties voted in favour, and assume that the opinions expressed by the Devon and Midlands delegates truly represented the feelings of clubs in their respective areas, it becomes apparent (after some simple arithmetic) that not less than 22 Yorkshire junior clubs voted against their own county executive's proposal. This allows for Yorkshire's own vote and their four representatives on the Rugby Union committee. Of course, if clubs in other parts of the country did support the motion, then this could only mean that many more Yorkshire clubs were opposed to the prospect of broken-time being paid by their rich neighbours.

In fact, this opposition from the junior organisations, many of which took less annually in gate-money than some senior clubs spent on snow-clearing, had been predicted by Frank Marshall in 1891, when he stated:

*Payment for broken-time, then, is a scheme so manifestly to the interest of the great clubs and prejudicial to the smaller clubs, that there is very little chance of a majority of votes being polled in its favour.*

With the unlikely prospect of the kind of proportional representation which was referred to in the first chapter, namely, one based on club membership or gate receipts, the senior northern gate-taking clubs were always going to be at loggerheads with what *"Old Ebor"* called *"tin-pot organisations"*. What, then, was their reaction to the above defeat, which, although widely anticipated, nonetheless created an atmosphere of unease within the game?

All talk of disunion, prior to and during the meeting at the Westminster Palace Hotel, appears to have from the amateur zealots in the north, such as Frank Marshall and Roger Walker, and, of course, from leading figures in the south, such as Rowland Hill and Arthur Budd, the latter who, incidentally, was a notable absentee from the crucial debate, having emigrated to South Africa. In the unlikely event of broken-time having been passed, there was every prospect that the defeated party would have formed themselves into the equivalent of *"Pa"* Jackson's Amateur Football Association. There was no indication, however, that the north's leading exponents had any immediate plans to secede from the Rugby Union. They were, it seems, quite prepared to bide their time.

This is what *The Yorkshire Post* [21] had to say in the aftermath of Yorkshire's defeat:

*It is unfortunate that sportsmen of the south are inexperienced in the difficulties under which football is conducted in the north. The latter has long ago outstripped the south in the number and capacity of its clubs and players, and we are convinced that the future support and progress of rugby in England must be looked for more in Lancashire and Yorkshire than in all the other parts of the country put together. That being so, it is important to note that the leading clubs of the north, are unanimously in favour of the concession which the Yorkshire Union proposed. To ignore an expression of opinion form such a body of clubs is unwise, and, viewed as a matter of tactics, a mistake.*

*Whatever southerners may say, it is in these clubs that the future development of the game has to be looked for, and on that ground alone it is unwise to act and speak as if it would be a desirable thing for the northern clubs to accede from the present union and form a combination of their own. Those people who glibly talk of such a course can have little idea of the effect of it upon the Rugby Union.*

*The Union would be a very sorry body indeed minus the membership of the great clubs of Yorkshire and Lancashire. We are glad to know that there is no serious danger of secession being suggested by Yorkshire. Foolish remarks of that sort have mostly come from the other side; in other words, from the side which would be chiefly damaged by the realisation of its own suggestion. Beaten at the poll, Yorkshire will certainly adhere loyally to the English Union for the general good of rugby football....*

These cautionary words, however, were written without the knowledge that a further crisis was already in the making, at the heart of which was the Reverend Frank Marshall himself. When it is realised that during the days leading up to the broken-time meeting, from the 16th to the 18th of September, Frank Marshall had been the guest of the Cumberland President, Mr R. Westray, for the purpose of assisting the latter to bring a charge of *"kidnapping"* against his own club, Huddersfield, it is not that difficult to understand why the Almondbury headmaster was now alienated from most of Yorkshire rugby.

At the same time, uplifted by their success at the broken-time poll, some members of the southern rugby establishment were actually advocating that clubs which were found guilty of professionalism should not only be suspended, but permanently excluded from the Rugby Union. Huddersfield, therefore, largely on the evidence of Frank Marshall, were to be placed first in line for excommunication. If this had happened then the rest of the Yorkshire Senior Competition clubs would almost certainly have resigned in support.

In the next volume we shall see just how near the north came in 1893 to such a disunion, and how Reverend Marshall was finally hoisted by his own petard.

# Notes

## Chapter One - Reverend Frank Marshall, B.A.

1   Gerald Hinchliffe, *A History of St. James' Grammar School in Almondbury* (1963).
2   75, Bridge Street, Wednesbury. The 1881 Census for 42, School Hill (St. Helens Gate), Almondbury, shows Sarah Marshall aged 66 as head of the household, Reverend Francis aged 35, Thomas Brown, an 18-year old assistant schoolmaster, born at Kirkheaton, two house maids, a cook and under cook. As well as 19 local scholars, aged 12-16, from the families of the middle-class of Huddersfield, there was also one born in Durham and five from Staffordshire. The 1891 Census shows Francis, aged 45, Catherine A. Marshall, his wife, aged 42, Sarah Marshall, aged 76, plus nine boarders, and two assistant schoolmasters, including one from Walsall in Staffordshire.
3   *The Yorkshire Post,* 15 November, 1893.
4   *The Yorkshireman,* October, 1890.
5   *The Yorkshire Post,* 14 October, 1889. Speech by Reverend Marshall at the annual dinner of the Dewsbury & Savile F.C. at the Masonic Hall, Longcauseway, on 11 October, 1889.
6   George F. Berney, *Progress of the Rugby Football Union from 1892-3 to the Present Time* in Leonard R. Tosswill (ed.) *Football: The Rugby Union Game* (1925).
7   Reverend Marshall's father-in-law was John Edward Taylor (J. E. Taylor & Bros, Birks Mill).
8   Reverend Marshall made a speech at the Carmarthen Training College reunion which was held at the Griffin Hotel, Leeds on 20 February, 1892.
9   Cambridge University Library, Department of Manuscripts and University Archives.
10  Reverend F. Marshall, *Football: The Rugby Union Game* (1892).
11  Percy M. Young, *History of British Football* (1968).
12  F. W. Hackwood, *Wednesbury Football Reminiscences* in *Ryders Annual* (1907); Charles Marshall, of John Jessop, Miles and Marshall, 7a Imperial Arcade, New Street, Huddersfield, lived at Grove House, Honley in 1884. The office moved to 36, New Street, Huddersfield by 1891. By 1897 he was Registrar to the Holmfirth County Court and lived at West View.
13  Percy Morris, *Aston Villa - The History of a Great Football Club 1874-1960* (1960).
14  The assumption of Reverend Marshall's illness is made due to a reference in *The Watchword* (Huddersfield), November, 1891.
15  *The Almondburian,* 1891.
16  Reverend F. Marshall, *Athletic News Annual 1891/2.*
17  *The Yorkshire Post,* 23 September, 1893.
18  *The Yorkshireman,* September, 1893.

## Chapter Two - The North-South Divide?

1   Stanley Chadwick, *Claret and Gold* (1946).
2   *Almondburian,* February, 1889.
3   Yorkshire's first-ever President of the Rugby Union, Harry Wharfedale Garnett, a paper manufacturer of Otley, was educated at Blackheath

Proprietary School.

4   Percy M. Young, *A History of British Football* (1968).
5   Michael E. Ulyatt and Bill Dalton, *Old Faithful, A History of Hull Football Club 1865-1987* (1988).
6   Terry Godwin, *The Complete Who's Who of International Rugby* (1987).
7.  *The Bradford Observer*, 11 March, 1895.
8   *The Times*, 26 April, 1928.
9   *The Yorkshire Post*, 28 September, 1891
10  Reverend F. Marshall, *Football: The Rugby Union Game* (1892).
11  Geoffrey Best, *Mid-Victorian Britain, 1851-75*, in E. Hobsbawn (ed.), *The History of British Society* (1971).
12  Stuart Barlow, *The Diffusion of Rugby Football in the Industrialized Context of Rochdale, 1868-90: A Conflict of Ethical Values*, in *The International Journal of the History of Sport* (April, 1993).
13  *Almondburian* February, 1889.
14  Trevor Delaney, *The Grounds of Rugby League* (1991).
15  Eric Dunning and Kenneth Sheard, *Barbarians, Gentlemen and Players : A Sociological Study of the Development of Rugby Football* (1979).
16  *The Yorkshire Post*, 12 October, 1886.
17  *The Yorkshire Post*, 17 April, 1891.
18  *Durham Chronicle*, 15 April, 1892.
19  Marshall p 96.
20  Marshall pp 323 and 329.
21  "Nomad", *The Future of Rugby Football: Professionalism and the League"* in *The Yorkshireman Football Number 1892*.
22  Fred Lister, *History of (Hartlepool) Rovers 1879-1979* (1979).
23  *Chats with Celebrated Yorkshire Footballers Number 4* (   ).
24  *The Yorkshire Post*, 31 October, 1882.
25  *The Yorkshire Post*, 28 September, 1891.
26  *The Yorkshire Post*, 28 September, 1891. It should be noted, however, that at Lancashire's AGM on 15 September, 1891, J. W. Clegg (Wigan) spoke in favour of the Yorkshire proposal.

## Chapter Three - Professionalism in other Sports

1   Ric Sissons, *The Players: A Social History of the Professional Cricketer* (1988).
2   Peter Wynne-Thomas, *"Give Me Arthur": A Biography of Arthur Shrewsbury* (1985).
3   David Frith, *"My Victorious Stod": A Biography of A. E. Stoddart* (   ).
4   William H. Hoole, *The Cricketing Squire*, (1991), and *Blackburn Times* 19 December, 1925, and *The Times* 18 December, 1925 and 21 December, 1925,
5   Marshall p404; and Robert Brooke and David Goodyear, *A Who's Who of Lancashire County Cricket Club* (   ).
6    Gerald Hinchliffe, *A History of St. James' Grammar School in Almondbury* (1963) and *Almonburian*, 1891; see also Sissons.
7   C. E. Sutcliffe and F. Hargreaves, *History of The Lancashire Football Association 1878-1928* (1928).

8    Percy M. Young, *A History of British Football* (1968).
9    Wray Vamplew, *Pay up and play the game: Professional sport in Britain, 1875-1914* (1988).
10   Dunning and Sheard p187.
11   Edward Grayson, *Corinthians and Cricketers* (1955).
12   Percy M. Young, *Football in Sheffield* (1962).
13   Grayson, pp107-108 quoting *"Pa"*Jackson in *Association Football* (   ).
14   Marshall p105.
15   Marshall p132.
16   *The Yorkshire Post*, 12 October, 1886
17   Paul Greenhalgh, *The Work and Play Principle: The Professional Regulations of the Northern Rugby Football Union, 1898-1905* in *The International Journal of the History of Sport*,(December, 1992).
18   Dunning and Sheard pp176-182.
19   *The Yorkshire Post*, 18 September, 1893.

## Chapter Four - Veiled Professionalism

1    *"A Wag"*, *The Yorkshireman Football Number, 1890.*
2    Reverend F. Marshall, *Athletic News Annual 1891/2.*
3    Reverend F. Marshall, *Football: The Rugby Union Game* (1892) p56.
4    *Durham Chronicle*, 5 May, 1893 refers to these statistics as being for the whole of Great Britain, whilst E. Dunning and K. Sheard, *Barbarians, Gentlemen and Players* (1979) p220, quoting the *Wakefield Express* 8 April, 1893, misinterpret these as being for Yorkshire only.
5    Michael E. Ulyatt and Bill Dalton, *Old Faithful, A History of Hull Football Club 1865-1987* (1988).
6    *The Yorkshire Post*, 3 October, 1886.
7    Marshall p107.
8    *The Yorkshire Post*, 10 February, 1890.
9    *Ibid.*, 19 May, 1893.
10   *Ibid.*, 20 January, 1890.
11   C. F. Shaw, *History of Batley: The Gallant Youths* (1899).
12   *The Dewsbury Reporter*, 6 January, 1912; and Tom Webb's *History of Oldham* in the club programmes during the 1967/8 season.
13   J.C. Lindley and D. W.Armitage, *100 Years of Rugby: The History of Wakefield Trinity 1873-1973* (1973).
14   *The Western Daily Mercury*, 15 February, 1913.
15   W. Garvin, *Warrington Centenary 1879-1979* (1979).
16   *"Athlete"* in *Oldham Chronicle Saturday Supplement*, 15 November, 1890.
17   David Smith and Gareth Williams, *Fields of Praise: The Official History of the Welsh Rugby Union 1881-1981* (1980).
18   *The Bradford Observer*, 9 March, 1892.
19   *Ibid.*, 3 March, 1886.
20   *The Yorkshire Post*, 12 October, 1886.
21   *Ibid.*, 3 October, 1886.
22   *Ibid.*, 26 September, 1891.

23  Trevor Delaney, *T'lads ower t'bridge: A History of Leeds Parish Church Recreation Club* in Issue 6 *Code 13,* March, 1988.

24  *The Bradford Observer,* 11 August, 1893.

25  *Ibid.,* 27 February, 1893.

26  Marshall p356.

27  Fred Lister, *History of (Hartlepool) Rovers 1879-1979* (1979).

28  *The Bradford Observer,* 25 September, 1893.

29  *Carlisle Patriot,* May, 1893.

30  *"A Wag" - The Yorkshireman Football Number, 1890.*

31  Ulyatt and Dalton p15 ; and Lindley and Armitage p16.

32  Gareth Williams, *How Amateur Was My Valley: Professional Sport and National Identity in Wales 1890-1914. The British Journal of Sports History, December, 1985* quoting H. H. Almond, *Football as a Moral Agent, Nineteenth Century,* December, 1893.

33  Nigel C. Starmer-Smith, *The Barbarians: The Official History of The Barbarian Football Club* (1977).

34  *The Yorkshireman,* September, 1893.

35  *The Yorkshire Post,* 11 March, 1893.

36  *Ibid.,* 13 March, 1893.

37  *The Bradford Observer,* 13 March, 1893.

## Chapter Five - The Tour of 1888

1  Arthur Shrewsbury's own letters; and Peter Wynne-Thomas, *"Give Me Arthur": A Biography of Arthur Shrewsbury* (1985).

2  *Keighley News,* 14 January, 1888.

3  *Ibid.,* 7 January, 1888.

4  *Ibid.,* 14 January, 1888.

5  *The Yorkshire Post,* 1 March, 1888 and 19 March, 1888.

6  Reverend F. Marshall, *Football: The Rugby Union Game* (1892) p502.

7  *The Yorkshire Post,* 8 March, 1888.

8  John Griffiths, *British Lions* (1990), who also refers to the fact that Harry Speakman stayed in Australia and later captained Queensland.

9  *The Yorkshire Post,* 19 March, 1888.

10  Griffiths p16.

11  On 13 December, 1890, John Nolan, *"late beerhouse keeper of Coronation Arms, Mumps",* was sued by a Samuel Holt Lord for injury to his left eye and was subsequently fined £50 with costs. Nolan is not listed in the 1891 *Kelly's* trade directory, presumably having failed to obtain another license. He died in 1907 following an accident at his work in Dukinfield.

12  C. F. Shaw, *History of Batley: The Gallant Youths* (1899).

13  *The Yorkshire Post,* 24 February, 1888.

14  *Ibid.,* 5 October, 1888.

15  Marshall p504.

16  *Minutes of the Rugby Football Union,* 15 November, 1888.

17  A. M. C. Thorburn, *The Scottish Rugby Union Official History* (1980).

18  Swinton played the tourists on Monday, 4 February, 1889, in a benefit match

for Seddon's youngest brother. A crowd of 6,000 saw Kent score the only try of the match for the tourists, who, interestingly, had Clowes in their side. Clowes left for an African tour in August 1890, but later returned to Halifax and played for that club in the Northern Union.

19   *The Athletic News Annual* 1894/5.
20   Wynne-Thomas p107; see also Ric Sissons, *The Players: A Social History of the Professional Cricketer* (1988).

## Chapter Six - Professional Inquiries prior to the 1893 Broken-Time Meeting

1   *Yorkshire Football*, 24 January, 1888.
2   Arthur Budd, *The Future of the Rugby Game* in the *Athletic News Football Annual 1895/6.*
3   *"A Pro. in Mufti"*, *Professional Football: A Plea for Legitimate Concessions* in *The Yorkshireman Football Number, March, 1891.*
4   *The Yorkshire Post,* 2 October, 1888.
5   *Ibid.,* 13 November, 1888.
6   *Ibid.,* 24 December, 1888.
7   *"Athlete"*, *Rugby Football and Professionalism* in the *Oldham Saturday Supplement,* 15 November, 1890.
8   *The Yorkshire Post,* 20 February, 1889.
9   *Ibid.,* 16 July, 1889 and 20 July, 1889.
10   *Ibid.,* 20 September, 1889.
11   *Ibid.,* 17 January, 1890.
12   *Ibid.,* 28 September, 1889; and Percy M. Young, *Bolton Wanderers (1965).*
13   *The Yorkshire Post,* 21 January, 1890.
14   *The Yorkshire Post,* 10 February, 1890.
15   *The Oldham Evening Chronicle,* 29 September, 1890.
16   *The Oldham Saturday Standard,* 25 October, 1890; *The Oldham Evening Chronicle,* 25 October, 1890; and *The Yorkshire Post,* 30 October, 1890; in 1895 David Gwynn was licensee of the Prince William of Gloucester, 7 Market Place and West Street, Oldham.
17   Joseph Platt, the Northern Union's first secretary, had been a member of the Oldham club from 1880. A qualified land surveyor, he was a partner in Platt & Whipp, surveyors and accountants, the managing-director of the Empire Theatre of Varieties Co. Ltd, which owned a number of theatres in Oldham, as well as being a director of Fernhurst Spinning Companies, and Wild & Co. Ltd., billposters.
18   *The Yorkshire Post,* 20 April, 1891.
19   *The Bradford Observer,* 10 November, 1891.
20   David Smith and Gareth Williams, *Fields of Praise: The Official History of the Welsh Rugby Union 1881-1981* (1980).
21   Reverend F. Marshall, Football: *The Rugby Union Game* (1892) pp 516 and 517.
22   *The Yorkshire Post,* 3 April, 1893.
23   *The Yorkshireman,* April, 1893.
24   *The Bradford Observer,* 9 March, 1892.

25 *Durham Chronicle,* 21 and 28 October, 1892, and 15 September, 1893; Wheatley was reinstated to play for Houghton for the start of the 1893/4 season. As Rockcliff were also involved, details were sent to Northumberland County who later exonerated that club.

26 *The Yorkshire Post,* 11 November, 1892.

27 *Ibid.,* 16 March, 1893.

28 *Ibid.,* 6 and 7 December, 1892.

29 *Ibid.,* 9 December, 1892.

30 Gerald Hinchliffe, *A History of St. James' Grammar School in Almondbury* (1963).

## Chapter Seven – The Great Debate

1 *The Yorkshire Post,* 20 February, 1889.

2 Eric Dunning and Kenneth Sheard, *Barbarians, Gentlemen and Players: A Sociological Study of the Development of Rugby Football* (1979) p150.

3 *The Yorkshire Post,* 23 September, 1893.

4 *Blackburn Times,* 14 September, 1893; and *Keighley News,* 16 September, 1893.

5 "Old Ebor" *The Yorkshire Alliance Movement* in *Athletic News Football Annual 1892/3;* this obviously did not include Devonians who formed a league for the 1892/3 season.

6 *The Yorkshire Post,* 6 May, 1889.

7 For example, the West Lancashire League commenced in 1889-90.

8 "Athlete," in *Oldham Chronicle Saturday Supplement,* 15 November, 1890.

9 *The Yorkshire Post,* 20 July, 1892.

10 *Ibid.,* 23 August, 1892.

11 "Old Ebor," *The Yorkshire Alliance Movement* in *Athletic News Football Annual 1892/3.*

12 *The Yorkshire Post,* 15 September, 1892; and "Philistine," *Leagues in Rugby Football - What Lancashire Has Done.*

13 *The Yorkshire Post,* 11 April, 1891.

## Chapter Eight  -  The Broken-Time Meeting - "A Triumph for Veiled Professionalism"

1 D. Taylor and D. Bush, *The Golden Age of British Hotels* (1974); and Priscilla Boniface, *Hotels and Restaurants 1830 to the Present Day* (1981). The Westminster Palace Hotel coffee room was said to have been 98 feet long by 30 feet wide. The hotel, which was later converted into offices and renamed Abbey House, was demolished in the 1970s.

2 George F. Berney, *Progress of the Rugby Football Union from 1892-3 to the Present Time* in Leonard R. Tosswill (ed.) *Football: The Rugby Union Game (1925).*

3 Boniface.

4 At the time of the meeting William Cail, an analytical chemist, was head of Cail & Partners, import and export merchants, and was also managing-director of Cail Bitmo Co. Ltd. Educated in Germany, in his younger days he had been a centre three-quarter, as well as being an expert yachtsman and a champion oarsman.

5 The summary of the meeting is based on reports in *The Bradford Observer* and

The Times, 21 September, 1893; *The Yorkshire Post*, 21 September, 1893; the *Stalybridge Reporter* and *Wakefield Express*, 23 September, 1893; and *Pastime*, 27 September, 1893.

6   The future Mayor of Macclesfield, and future President of the Rugby Union, Lieut-Colonel John Walter Hook Thorp was head of one of the oldest silk firms in England.

7   J. H. Fallas, who was appointed Wakefield Trinity secretary in December, 1892, was a cabinet manufacturer, and should not be confused with Herbert Fallas, Trinity's former international, an accountant, who was then clerk to Ossett Corporation.

8   *Stalybridge Reporter*, 23 September, 1893.

9   F. Innes Currey, the Old Marlburian solicitor and President of the Rugby Union 1884-6.

10  Tosswill p59.

11  *Pastime*, 23 September, 1893.

12  *Ibid.*

13  Minutes of the Rugby Football Union, September General Meeting, 20 September, 1893.

14  *The Bradford Observer*, 11 September, 1893.

15  *Bradford Daily Telegraph*, 23 September, 1893

16  Minutes of the Rugby Football Union, September General Meeting, 20 September, 1893.

17  Cheshire's AGM, which was held in Liverpool on 18 September, 1893, unanimously decided to instruct their delegates to oppose the broken-time proposal.

18  "*Amateur*", *Professionalism in Rugby* in the *Athletic News Football Annual 1898/99*,

19  *The Bradford Observer*, 21 September, 1893.

20  *Rochdale Times*, 23 September, 1893.

21  *The Yorkshire Post*, 23 September, 1893.

157

# Index

Printed by Thornton & Pearson (Printers) Ltd., Rosse Street, Thornton Road, Bradford BD8 9AS
Tel: 0274 487085